City in the Osage Hills

City in the Osage Hills

Tulsa, Oklahoma

Courtney Ann and Glen Vaughn-Roberson

PRUETT PUBLISHING COMPANY
Boulder, Colorado

First Edition
1 2 3 4 5 6 7 8 9

Printed in the United States of America

Library of Congress Cataloging in Publication Data

Vaughn-Roberson, Courtney Ann, 1949–
City in the Osage Hills.

Bibliography: p.
Includes index.
1. Tulsa (Okla.)–History. 2. Tulsa (Okla.)–Social conditions. I. Vaughn-Roberson, Glen, 1946–
II. Title.
F704.T92V38 1983 976.6'86 82-24062
ISBN 0-87108-644-1

ACKNOWLEDGMENTS

Many people have helped us in this effort, and we could not possibly acknowledge everyone. We do wish to give special thanks to the staff of the Oklahoma State University Library for its consistently friendly assistance; to the employees of the Tulsa Chamber of Commerce, especially Bruce Carnett, who not only opened the files but also extended us a warm welcome; and to M. Hettie Green, secretary for the Tulsa City Commissioners, who graciously allowed us to rummage through city ordinances and commission proceedings. We deeply appreciate, also, the tireless typing and editorial aid of Lois Broady.

CONTENTS

INTRODUCTION

The Historical Perspective

The history of Tulsa, Oklahoma, (beginning with sixteenth-century Creek Tallahassee) is similar to many other western city stories because it symbolizes a blending of individual initiative and community cooperative planning. Yet lay historians and a large number of scholars have emphasized the former at the expense of the latter and portrayed the western settlers as the yeoman farm family, or lone persons, living a solitary life on the American frontier. The stereotype originated in medieval Europe, crossed the Atlantic with the first English and Spanish settlers, and imbued the political and social philosophies of men like Thomas Jefferson. In the eighteenth and nineteenth centuries fur trappers, explorers, Indian scouts, and buffalo hunters achieved immortality from the pens of essayists, poets, and historians who were enamored with the myth that isolated persons, not groups of settlers, settled the West. In addition, many readers think of western cities as boom towns, the overnight products of mineral discoveries and land runs. Their lasting existence, however, was due to tremendous communal efforts. In the nineteenth and twentieth centuries black slaves (later freedmen), cattle barons, and oil people were the first to threaten the old stability and infiltrate homogeneous Creek Tallahassee, first located in Alabama and then removed to Indian Territory during the 1820s and '30s. Although the separatist Indians lost in the ensuing confrontations, townspeople worked out their differences. Ironically, during the 1880s, as scholar Frederick Jackson Turner bemoaned the disappearance of free and open lands, as the subsequent safety valve for American democracy and individualism, a new breed of pioneers migrated to Tallahassee. They saw very little financial future in a lawless conglomeration of peoples and introduced communal cooperation, the new phase of advancing civilization. Later known as Tulsa, Indian Territory, the town ultimately has become a modern urban center in Oklahoma because Progressive-Era civic leaders and their progeny, throughout the 1900s, planned and promoted industrial development and cultural enrichment projects.

This case study suggests additional support for the classic Stanley Elkins-Eric McKitrick proposition voiced in "A Meaning for Turner's Frontier." They propose that American frontier boosters exemplified the Turner contention that the challenges of a rugged environment evoked strength and leadership. We cannot, however, discount the conflict framework proposed by Robert Dykstra in *The Cattle Towns* or Allan Bogue in "Social Theory and the Pioneer." They emphasize the increased conflict that infested any town nestled in an unsettled area. Historiographically our work's perspective is most in line with that of Don Harrison Doyle in *The Social Order of a Frontier Community*. He accepts the Dykstra or Bogue interpretation as a framework, but he concludes a consensus between the two opposing theories. Doyle admonishes the reader that although western settlements were beset with strife, scholars must not promote the scenario of a constantly unstable setting and ignore the fact that conflict also spawned democratic decision making and a social order. He states:

> In its paradoxical combinations of nobility and stability, voluntarism and collective discipline, Jacksonville's social order seemed to strike a workable compromise between the chaos of an expansive capitalist society and the enduring human need for community.

While turmoil did exist in Tulsa and at times dominated a given setting, citizens managed to institutionalize their disputes through economics, politics, education, religion, and service groups. Although they usually accommodated each other, there were always those whose poverty or powerlessness made them outcasts. Even so, democratic or progressive processes of cooperation (led only sometimes by boosters) have dominated Tulsa's growth, thereby illustrating that a person's need for communal security and/or economic prosperity will eventually force or inspire him or her to build a community.

Much of the literature on western community life remains yet to be written, and Tulsa's past is no exception. Few persons have authored books about the city, and all available materials are either dated and out of print or done in a cursory fashion. Clarence B. Douglas's *The History of Tulsa, Oklahoma: A City With Personality,* published in 1921, and James M. Hall's *The Beginning of Tulsa* are unscholarly memoirs of the early town. In 1943, noted historian Angie Debo wrote *From Creek Town to Oil Capital,* which is well composed, but her 200 pages concentrated primarily on the Creek Indian period and devoted only thirty pages to the community after 1910. Finally, two pictorial accounts complete the list–one, of the city's development, called *Tulsa 75: A History of Tulsa,* by William Butler, and another, on Tulsa architecture, entitled *Tulsa: An Architectural Era, 1925–1942,* by the Junior League of Tulsa. Numerous authors, however, have contributed both academic and popular articles to the *Chronicles of Oklahoma,* which we found very useful.

We did, however, unearth invaluable primary sources in city records: *Minutes of the Directors' Meetings of the Chamber of Commerce*; in the two major newspapers, *The Tulsa Tribune* (called the *Tulsa Daily Democrat* prior to 1920), and the *Tulsa Daily World;* as well as in journals or magazines of earlier days that contain timely articles concerning many aspects of social, economic, and political life in the city during the twentieth century.

I

Creek Tulsa

According to white recorded history, Tulsa began in the 1500s with European North American exploration and colonization and extended through the American Civil War. For at least these 300 years the progeny of Creek Nation Indians inhabited and sustained a commune in the continent's southeastern region. To escape the impending foreign intervention, they transported their dwellings twice. First, early in the nineteenth century, they journeyed to a secluded spot within the Creek jurisdiction, which the United States had dubbed Alabama, and again during the 1830s, 1,000 miles west, to what we know now as Oklahoma. By the late 1860s, however, the first Tulsans found that they could not escape those who sought to control them and their town, thus ending the three-century-old era of Creek Tulsa.

Once a settlement resting on the swiftly flowing Tallapoosa riverbank in the present state of Alabama, the small, quiet Creek village provided personal and economic protection for scores of Indians. The date of its founding is lost in unrecorded history, but the first people to write of this place belonged to a 1541 Spanish expedition led by adventurer Hernando de Soto. As Governor of Cuba, de Soto had a commission from the Spanish authorities to explore and conquer the unknown, loosely defined area called Florida, and while he and 600 soldiers were carrying out this grant they stumbled into the town.

The Spaniards found that, as in any other settlement, the early Tulsans formed their community for mutual protection and prosperity. They held communal lands which designated citizens farmed. Even in the sixteenth century, Tallahassee (meaning "old town" in Creek) was well established. Nested on the edge of a forest, its buildings were constructed of lumber cemented with hardened riverbed clay. In traditional Creek style, all structures encompassed a village square in which people performed religious rituals or commingled with travelers from neighboring tribes. De Soto thought it a central governing point for outlying villages.

The Creeks divided their nation into two geographical districts. Tallahassee's location was among the Lower Creeks, who existed largely in the present state of Alabama, while the Upper Creeks resided in today's Georgia. Both sent representatives to the General Council, a national governmental body, but conducted their affairs independently of each other. The two divisions functioned identically; however, each was as a confederation of towns loosely joined together for protection against sporadic warfare conducted with Indian tribes–Catawba, Iroquois, Cherokee, and Shawnee–which inhabited the immediate north. Each community was virtually autonomous, but the village chiefs did hold annual regional meetings in various locations, Tallahassee being one.

As mentioned, even though the federation was a decentralized body, a governmental hierarchy did exist. A head chief, who had only negligible powers as the presiding officer of the General Council, led the nation. Composed of one representative from each village, the Council functioned as an advisory body that formulated national policies and suggested government regulations, such as intertribal trade. Its aegis, however, extended to discussing only inter-village relations and diplomatic ventures with the outside world. Messengers from the Council orally reported all agreements to the villages, not as laws, but as recommendations, and the adherence of many communities was mercurial. Even during wartime each town judicially guarded its autonomy. If the tribe conducted military campaigns, the Council appointed a temporary chief who was a stronger national leader than was the peacetime head. Even so, the General Council's power was so limited that various towns often failed to support a war effort. Thus, although Creeks were known as well-trained, fierce soldiers, they were notoriously ineffective against well-organized opposition and rarely enjoyed numerical superiority. Thus ironically, clans who lived in Tallahassee or elsewhere, jealously shielding their local independence, were often unable to protect themselves from the influence of invaders.

The ideal, self-sufficient local structure to which the Creeks clung so fervently represented generations of tradition that serviced the peoples' economic and physical survival needs. One or more clans lived in each village in which a town council, headed by a chief or minko, made major decisions. Usually the minko was the leader of the numerically largest clan and preferably the next-of-kin within his predecessor's maternal lineage. Creeks proportioned council representation according to the relative population of each clan which had at least one vote. In contrast to the arbitrary enforcement of tribal edicts, those that the town council made the inhabitants obeyed. Locals viewed these rulings as pertinent to their immediate needs; thus they taught each generation a strong sense of communal obligation. Each clan perceived its individual members' actions as a reflection of the group, and unacceptable behavior brought disgrace to a family.

Local government served both military and civil functions among the clans. Civil administration officials, chosen from families who traditionally governed a community during times of peace, decided matters concerning cultivation of collectively owned fields, erection of public buildings, relations with neighboring towns, and other projects of civic concern. During war, when the Creeks had a national leader, local military administrators controlled the village. When the town was at peace they served as a police force, apprehending those who violated laws that the council established. The Creeks' political system lasted until after the Civil War, at which time they decided to install a more democratic and organized government, blueprinted from the United States Constitution.

Until the Indians became "Americanized" the only need they detected for a centralized government was to provide warriors for the perpetual conflicts, but even then battle heroes were locally, not nationally, decorated. Constant intertribal strife promoted the growth of a strong soldier class. Early in their history the Creeks instituted war titles, and every young man dreamed of someday being revered as a resourceful leader and courageous fighter. Nevertheless, before a male achieved soldier status he had to pass a series of demanding tests that required years of preparation and training; even the initiation rites lasted from four to eight months. The three higher titles–leader, upper leader, and great warrior–represented battlefield citations. A town's minko conferred such distinctions after receiving the advice and consent of a village council. Although every community had several men ranking in the second and third echelons, only one person at a time bore the title "great warrior." The holder of this cherished designation had both social and political prestige. When the council decided to negotiate a diplomatic dispute, rather than fight, the great warrior could supercede the decision and lead those who would follow him into battle.

Because men were crucial to the defense of individual Creek settlements such as Tallahassee, women took a subordinate role within the social structure. Although Creeks chose a minko through the maternal family lineage, a woman's primary function was to provide her clan with children, preferably males. Her other duties included harvesting grain, weaving cloth, and dressing game. She was not permitted to participate in the council, as females were considered incapable of making governmental decisions. Never could a woman argue with her father, brothers, or husband, and these men expected her to act in the most modest manner. Women, however, did play a major role when it came to mate selection, either for themselves or for their daughters. No courting was done without consent of the mother and the maternal uncle. A prospective husband sought approval by presenting suitable gifts to the girl's mother, grandmother, and aunts. The young people exercised some degree of choice, but no girl married without approval from the female members of her family. After a simple ceremony, the newlyweds lived with the wife's family until the husband built a home of their own.

Marriage was a sacred institution. Divorce was uncommon, and adultery was a serious crime restricted by severe punishment. The Creeks practiced polygamy; however, the husband took a second wife only after obtaining consent from the first. Occasionally he married a sister-in-law, especially if the woman was in her declining "eligible years." Unattached females eighteen or older were considered abnormal and of questionable virtue, or carriers of evil demons; shame was their lot and that of their family. A dutiful brother-in-law, therefore, might remove the stigma by marrying such a woman. Seldom did a man have more than two wives, for only the most prosperous could financially support several spouses and the brood that followed.

The Creek families anchored an agrarian society. The staple diet consisted of grains supplemented with fish and fresh meat. Periodic harvests from the family garden, in which various vegetables were nurtured, sustained the tribe. Certain families farmed the communal lands and stored the harvest both in public granaries and in individual homes. The council then apportioned the food according to need. The village chief periodically commissioned large hunting parties to search for meat and hides, which the townspeople consumed or traded, although the General Council sometimes attempted to regulate and in some cases prohibit commerce with neighboring tribes.

Such was the life among the first Tulsans and many of the other Creek community residents until whites began to descend upon their land during the eighteenth century. The Indians realized too late that European colonization of North America mandated that the Creek Nation adopt a new socio-political organization that subordinated the towns to a central government authority. Only a tightly governed tribe could have forced locally rooted clans to recognize the need for collaboration, not aggression, between themselves and surrounding fellow Indians in order to unite against the inevitable wave of white settlers. These visions, however, were difficult to conjure because during the European colonial period the Creek confederacy remained sufficiently cohesive to protect tribal territory and to deal with foreigners on terms favorable to the Indians. After the American Revolution, during President George Washington's first administration, the Upper Creeks became increasingly disturbed by the ambitious new country's settlers and alarmed by more progressive, neighboring Lower Creek tribes which began ceding land to American citizens.

As the threat continued, political and social differences emerged between Upper and Lower Creeks. Although Tallahassee belonged to the more progressive of the two Creek divisions, many of the townspeople held that the purpose of a community was to preserve ancient cultural and economic practices by shunning outsiders. Sometime during the eighteenth century a group of them (who would later found Tulsa, in 1836) departed from Tallahassee and formed an offshoot town named Lochapoka, largely because they disagreed with the Creek national policy of allowing non-Creeks to incorporate into the Confederacy. The view that survival lay only in isolation was not a highly insightful opinion, because the progressive Lower Creek Nation, of which the Lochapoka residents were still a part, noted the inevitability of adapting to a culture of mixed races and nationalities. In retrospect, however, neither philosophy benefited the Creeks because United States citizens were never satisfied to merely share and assimilate with indigenous cultures. Instead, the fair-skinned European descendants eventually insisted on the extermination or total subjugation of their Indian brothers.

Other tribesmen besides the Lochapoka also wandered in search of new regions that would protect them from an inevitable future. Some Creeks migrated as far as Florida. These dissenters became "Seminole," a word meaning "people who camp in the distance." By the second decade of the nineteenth century the United States government, out of necessity, began to deal with the Florida tribes as separate from the Creek Nation.

No corner of the North American continent was far enough removed to provide shelter from men such as Major General Andrew Jackson from Tennessee who, against United States Army orders, in 1809 took bands of vigilantes and routed out many Seminoles and runaway slaves from Spanish-owned Florida. Bands of militant Upper Creeks, determined to insulate their nation from white encroachment, in 1811 joined the Shawnee Chief Tecumseh, who attempted to unite all Indians into a powerful confederation. The governor of the Ohio Valley, William Henry Harrison, aborted the plan at the Battle of Tippecanoe Creek in November of 1811. Tecumseh was not present, but here many of his followers died. Henceforth, Creek strength waned in the Southeast, and the Shawnee chief died a year later fighting for the British in the War of 1812. Like Tecumseh, many of the more conservative Creeks also fought for the British until Jackson, this time with the full seal of approval of the United States government, crushed most of the Upper Creek opposition and eventually forced them to bequeath 23 million acres to the newly proclaimed Americans. As a result, the General Council met in May 1824 and passed a law making the sale of tribal land punishable by death.

Peacetime brought even more settlers into Creek domains, and Chief William McIntosh, of the progressive Lower Creeks, began to realize that the best solution was to accept a United States offer of new land and a chance for a secluded home west of the Mississippi River, in the present state of Oklahoma. Many Upper Creeks hated McIntosh, who had negotiated and signed treaties with the United States government in 1802, 1814, and 1821, ceding large amounts of tribal holdings. Even within the Lower Creek district there was probably no love lost between McIntosh and many of the Lochapoka citizens, who also cherished their segregated community. Even though the various Creek towns exercised much independence in local matters, they faded in significance when posed against the fledgling, but ever growing, United States. Encouraged by McIntosh's compliance, early in 1825 President James Monroe sent two representatives to Georgia to formulate a final agreement that would remove the entire Creek Nation from the state. The meetings proved unsuccessful, for after much heated debate the General Council voted not to sell more territory. McIntosh and a few of his followers thereupon covertly agreed to meet with the commissioners at Indian Springs to continue discussing the question of removal. This second meeting convened in February 1825 despite repeated warnings by the General Council that acceptance of any terms uprooting Creeks from Georgia violated the law of 1824, which prohibited the sale of additional Creek land; yet, on February 12, 1825, McIntosh signed the treaty, which included an acre-for-acre exchange of all Georgia and Alabama possessions for territory in the Arkansas Valley and payment of $400,000 to the Creeks for expenses incurred while moving. Greed might have prompted McIntosh's outright defiance of the General Council, for he also obtained $25,000 from the United States government for his home and property. During the negotiations for previous treaties he had vehemently fought for and received guarantees that his holdings would not be included in the final agreements.

As a result of the settlement many Creeks loathed McIntosh, but in his defense one must note that he, also, gave up some of the richest acres in the Creek Nation and eighty of his own slaves. Perhaps this time the pot was sufficiently sweetened to change his mind, or maybe McIntosh recognized that the Creeks could not indefinitely stave off the United States and decided to accept the white men's offer before they took his land by force. In any event, the General Council wasted little time in finding him guilty of violating the law of 1825 and sentenced him to death. Early on the morning of April 30, 1825 his fellow chief, Menerva, and 100 braves executed McIntosh and burned his home. Meanwhile, on March 7, 1825, the new president of the United States, John Quincy Adams, had announced the Indian Springs Treaty. Reports of McIntosh's questionable actions began crossing the President's desk, and eventually he decided against the legality and authority of the document and invited the Lower Creeks to come to Washington to negotiate a new one.

On April 22, 1826, participants signed a settlement declaring the Treaty of Indian Springs null and void and announcing new terms more favorable to the Indians. The Upper Creeks ceded portions of their land in Georgia for $217,000 and a perpetual annuity of $20,000. For future purchase of territory, the United States agreed to pay a total of $430,000 and another $100,000 for the expense of moving west the followers of Chief McIntosh. Approximately two years later the first 780 Lower Creek migrants left the Southeast aboard a steamboat, *Fidelity,* bound for Three Forks, on the Arkansas River. Before the end of 1830 an additional 2,000 Lower Creeks joined them, but the determined Lochapokas were not among them. Many of the first Indian pioneers were wealthy mixed-bloods (white and Indian) who owned slaves and subscribed to individual land ownership; consequently, they built large plantations in Indian Territory and created a socio-economic life style similar to that of white Southwesterners.

The more militant Lower Creeks, in concert with the Lochapokas, protested longer than did many of the others against adopting white ways. On March 28, 1836, however, United States diplomatic tribal chiefs met at Lochapoka and made arrangements for yet thousands more remaining Lower and most of the Upper Creek warriors and their families to trek toward Indian Territory, carrying government-issued rifles, blankets, and ammunition. Added to this meager ration was the promise of a $3,000 annual education grant for twenty years and enough money to hire a blacksmith.

All five of the Civilized Tribes experienced what became known as the "Trail of Tears." Suffering from hunger, exposure, and disease, the Indians moved overland toward the West. An uprising among die-hard Upper Creeks in Alabama was understandable but further aggravated the ordeal. White settlers, eager to lay claim to the fertile area, had swarmed onto Creek land prior to the removal date. In desperation the Lochapokas joined other Upper Creeks and raided nearby Columbus, Alabama. The frontiersmen counterattacked, driving the Indians into the swamps and burning Tallahassee and Lochapoka. Demoralized by the onslaught, modern Tulsa's ancestors finally joined the stream of refugees without a backward glance and silently marched to a new, unfamiliar land across the Mississippi into the Osage Hills of Indian Territory.

No tribe suffered more from the ravages of war than did the Creeks, for their population declined more than 40 percent between 1830 and 1836. Even so, in the last year of the decline a small band of Lochapokas arrived at the bend of the Arkansas River in southeastern Indian Territory. According to legend, the diseased and impoverished people reverently built a sacred fire from wood they had carried from Alabama. A giant oak, which stands today at 1730 South Cheyenne Avenue, bears a bronze tablet to commemorate this solemn occasion–the founding of Tulsa.

The refugees constructed an approximate duplicate of old Lochapoka and christened it "Tallahassee." Buildings formed the town square, and the giant oak marked the southeast corner of the settlement. The pioneers cut down trees in the surrounding forest and dragged them to a designated spot along the west side of the square on which the men constructed a long, rectangular public building. Here the village council decided matters of general concern. On the south side stood the building in which civil administrators or members of the peace clans debated internal business, such as the direction of ceremonies, the organization of public works, and construction of community buildings. These leaders' families followed custom and erected their crude homes behind the south ediface, segregating members of the war clans to the north of the square. The young men who had not distinguished themselves as warriors lived in a row of buildings that faced west and formed the eastern border of the square.

As months went by, the little village filled the small clearing along the north bank of the river. The woods echoed with the sounds of men cutting trees and dragging fallen timber back to camp. Women transformed sod into communal farms and private gardens. The Creeks possessed only the crudest tools with which to build their new homes and plow earth hardened by thousands of years of undisturbed grass and foliage. Peeled saplings covered with clay composed the outside walls, and bark shingles served for roofs. Inside, the homes exhibited furnishings of hard, wooden chairs and makeshift beds; the less fortunate families slept on earthen floors. Women cooked meat and cornmeal in clay vessels over round, open stoves located in the center of the single room, and a hole cut in the roof allowed smoke to escape.

Like the "Trail of Tears" experience, the first few years hammered away at Creek courage and physical endurance. Although they planted crops immediately after arriving, Tallahasseeans had to survive until harvest. Federally licensed traders brought needed goods from Fort Gibson, but there was a dearth of guns and ammunition, needed commodities to the men's hunting and fishing efforts. Dishonest United States government contractors often withheld merchandise promised to dependent residents. On numerous occasions sellers lied to Washington officials about the amount of goods consigned to the Indians and received money for more than they delivered. Some United States Indian agents attempted to supervise all transactions and required independent traders to obtain permits; the profiteering continued, however. Such practices not only angered the Creeks but also frustrated honest whites.

In his annual report of 1857 to Commissioner of Indian Affairs John W. Denver, Southern Superintendent of Indian Affairs Elias Rector stated that there were numerous problems. One was that many Anglos and Indians disobeyed antiliquor laws. Only a strong United States Army or Indian police show of force would end the flow of smuggled liquor to the Creeks, he contended. To check the sale of contraband in Indian Territory, Rector recommended that Indian agents should serve as law commissioners or that the federal government should create district courts. He added that because few Creeks understood white laws there was need for competent legal advisors, and yet all persons who voluntarily lived within the Creek Nation should also be subject to Creek law. Implementing his proposals was a problem, because whites and mixed-bloods were citizens of two nations, Creek and the United States. They could therefore appeal to federal courts when Creek law did not suit them. Rector believed that this and other complications could be solved if all members of the Five Civilized Tribes should enter the Union as a territory. In the fall of 1860 the General Council sent a delegation to Washington to discuss possible remedies, but the outbreak of the Civil War prevented any resolutions.

Although difficulties continued, many Tallahassee citizens prospered. The 1836 Treaty of Fort Gibson, signed in Cherokee Nation, Indian Territory, authorized a payment in livestock valued at $50,000 from Washington as compensation for losses during removal. Even separatist-oriented Tallahasseeans, who resisted until the last, received $10,000. After the first year the size and number of cattle and horse herds increased because of the favorable climate and nutritious grass. The Indians added to their daily diet by picking wild berries in the woods, hunting the plentiful game, and embarking on extended buffalo hunts. What they did not consume they sold at Fort Gibson or at the Indian agency located near Three Forks, in the Creek Nation. A brisk trade of pelts and buffalo hides for needed goods from the outside world developed up and down the Canadian and Arkansas rivers. The commerce inevitably forced changes in Tallahassee's isolationist image by bringing closer ties with other peoples. Symbolically, the first post office was opened at Three Forks in 1843. In 1848 Lewis Perryman, a member of one Tulsa founding family, built a store at Tallahassee to which the locals carried pelts, corn, and nuts to exchange for bright cloth, farm tools, and ammunition. By 1850 a modicum of economic stability existed and lasted until the outbreak of the Civil War.

The War Between the States touched the lives of thousands in the Indian Territory, but no group of people suffered more than did the Creeks. Accentuating the two political divisions, the tribe contributed 1,675 men to the Union effort and 1,575 to the Confederates. Tallahasseeans sympathized with the Upper Creeks and the Seminoles, who fought for the Union under the direction of Chief Opothleyahola. Once again the nascent Tulsans acted in unison with a majority of the Upper Creeks. Ironically, these conservatives supported the more progressive Northern cause, rather than the agrarian, tradition-bound South, for a number of reasons. Primarily, Southerners had always been the ones who personally harassed and drove the Creeks from their homeland, even though the distantly located United States government usually sanctioned the entire process. In addition, each town pragmatically reasoned which belligerent would win and hoped for two events–that its choice would prove correct and that the victor would recognize the communities that had been loyal.

At the outset, Union forces under Opothleyahola organized an orderly retreat into Kansas; but close on their heels rode Southern general Colonel Douglas H. Cooper, a former Choctaw-Chickasaw Indian agent who commanded a large detachment of Choctaws and Chickasaws. The two forces finally clashed on November 19, 1861 at the Battle of Round Mountain. This first confrontation of the Civil War in the Indian Territory produced resounding victory for the Confederate troops. Opothleyahola's forces, disorganized, starving, and dying from exposure, fled into Kansas, not to return until the spring of 1862.

The ensuing violence was savage and destructive, for guerrilla tactics brought plundering, looting, and death. A few Creeks tried to remain neutral but were burned out and often shot. For instance, many Tallahassee civilians felt forced to abandon their town. Renegades stole large herds of cattle, drove them to Kansas railroad terminals and crowded them onto trains bound for eastern markets. At the end of the war a small band of Tallahassee people crossed the Kansas line and traveled the northeastern Creek Territory to return to their home. Little remained of the once peaceful settlement, however, because troops and looters had barbarically burned homes and buildings, and the sacred square was overgrown with grass and weeds, a sight that made even the strongest warrior weep. Once again the Indians faced the hardships of building anew.

Tallahassee witnessed a reconstruction policy designed to punish the vanquished. Indian Territory nations lost the western half of their effects, and here the United States government interned Plains Indians on newly formed reservations. Congress approved the procedure in 1863, and in the summer of 1865 the leaders of the various tribes received orders to meet by early September with United States commissioners at Fort Smith, in Arkansas. All five of the

Civilized Tribes sent emissaries. The American commission consisted of Dennis N. Cooley, a former United States Senator from Iowa; Colonel Ely Samuel Parker, General Ulysses S. Grant's military secretary; and Thomas Wister, a member of the Society of Friends. After discussions with Secretary of the Interior James Harlan, the commissioners departed for the fort, carrying instructions to obtain a peace treaty and negotiate new agreements superceding those signed with the Creeks prior to the Civil War. They were also to resolve animosities between both those who had remained loyal to the Union and those who had fought for the Confederacy. Slavery, of course, had to be abolished, and a new territorial government was to replace the ancient tribal political hierarchy.

On September 7 the two parties met. The following day Cooley announced that because various Indians had joined the Confederacy the old treaties were no longer valid. He stressed the gravity of the situation and expressed hope that the Creeks would sign new peace pacts as soon as possible. At that point he outlined the necessary stipulations for all future agreements. The agenda both dismayed and surprised the Creeks, because the Union Tallahassee representatives arrived expecting to outline a peace with the ex-Confederate faction, and their jurisdiction had favored the Union. They found, however, that the United States sought concessions from them, also. J. W. Dunn, Creek Nation federal agent and designated interpreter, advised Parker that the loyal Creeks resented being treated as if they had been the enemy and proceeded to tell Cooley that the followers of Opothleyahola had fled to Kansas, fighting a rearguard action all the way, and that in the spring of 1862 they had reorganized and fought throughout the war. Filled with desperation, Tallahassee delegates recalled that for generations their ancestors had resisted assimilation, fearful of losing everything with which they could identify, and yet now the federal government betrayed the progeny who attempted to live in harmony with the United States.

The ex-Confederate Creeks, also, added their own objections to the proposed treaty. Daniel Newman McIntosh, their spokesman, replied that they had no authority to sell tribal lands to the United States, so he requested time to confer with the General Council. He also objected to white enforcement of the Fourteenth

Amendment within the Creek Nation, because many of the Indians' former slaves now roamed free throughout the area, and he did not want the blacks to have political power; furthermore, he and his followers demanded compensation for the loss of their chattel bondsmen. In return, Confederate Creeks agreed to allot portions of Creek land for freedmen, but that was as far as they would go. After several days of negotiations, Creeks signed the peace treaty on United States terms; moreover, in January and February of 1866 the Nation authorized a second group of treaties, thereby ceding 3 million acres of land for relocation of Kansas Indians and granting a possible settlement for freedmen. Here, all ex-slaves gained citizenship within the Creek Nation. The federal government did take loyalist claims for losses during the war, and the tribe received money from the land sale to Kansas Indians and freedmen, but these were its only rewards.

The Creek Treaty of 1866 was significant for two reasons. First, the United States government viewed some Creeks' siding with the South as fomenting an "unprovoked war"; ironically, this was exactly what white settlers had done to the Creeks in Georgia and Alabama a few generations earlier. Secretary of the Interior Harlan, however, used the renewed hostilities to justify keeping a closer watch on tribal affairs. He forced the Creeks to agree to military occupation if the "need" should arise; thus the United States introduced police power within the Creek Nation. In addition, a minor clause in the 1866 treaty granted Congress the right to impose and establish territorial federal courts amid the Indians' governmental system, which years later directly challenged Creek law. Until statehood, numerous non-Creeks living within the tribe's domain were able to escape Creek authority by appealing to these courts.

In the years immediately following the war, Tallahassee played only a minor role in Creek politics, although it did support a reorganization of the Nation's government under a constitution adopted in 1867. Despite the distrust, apparently many Indians held that further attempts to imitate white society constituted their only hope of sustained existence. Even prior to the Civil War the progressive element, of which Tallahassee had become a part, was composed of many mixed-bloods. They had lobbied for a new system of Creek national government, but the conservatives had success-

Creek Council. (*Courtesy of The Thomas Gilcrease Institute of American History and Art, Tulsa, Oklahoma*)

fully blocked its passage. The old ways, composed of slowly moving, arbitrarily imposed edicts, impeded the transformation of Creek society from a rudimentary farm economy to a burgeoning commercial-agricultural center. Indian agent Major James W. Dunn, writing to the Department of Interior in 1867, outlined some of the problems:

> The laws as now administered, require four times the number of officers that would be necessary to execute properly and efficiently under a well-established code. These officers, whose numbers are scarcely known even to the authorities, are poorly paid, and are dissatisfied with their positions and salaries. Indeed, so imperfect is the government, that the duty of no officer is fully defined; so that it is difficult for them to determine when they attain or overstep their authority. They have many intelligent and energetic men among them who appreciate this position of affairs, and who are strongly urging reform.

Finally, in October of 1867, the General Council wrote a ten-article constitution designed to eliminate the evils. This organic law was similar to that of the United States, although a product of Creek tradition. In the preamble the signers declared: "In order

Stickball players. (*Courtesy of The Thomas Gilcrease Institute of American History and Art, Tulsa, Oklahoma*)

to form a more perfect union, establish justice, and secure to ourselves, and our children, the blessings of freedom, we, the people . . . do adopt the following constitution." Enfranchised male Creek Nation citizens elected a "Principal Chief of the Muskogee Nation" and a second man to head the executive branch.* Moreover, voters bestowed lawmaking power on a bicameral legislative council, divided into a "House of Kings" and a "House of Warriors." The upper house (Kings) retained one spokesman for each town, whom adult males elected for a term of four years. Members of the lower house (Warriors) also served four years, but each town elected at least one representative and additional ones for every 200 citizens. Finally, a man had to be thirty years old to hold any public office.

The constitution established a high court, composed of "five competent recognized citizens" who met each year on the first Monday in October. Judges had original jurisdiction over any case in which the damages were more than 100 dollars. Six district courts

*The Creek tribe was only one of several in the Muskogeean linguistic group.

heard litigations in which a defendant had the guaranteed trial by a jury of twelve "disinterested men."

Thus the Creeks created a republican system of government founded on the principles of "separation of powers," an indication that the white society was having an impact on the Creek Nation. Combined with a written code, the organic law represented a major change in political structure. The system lasted until statehood, in 1907, proving that Creeks were determined to live in harmony with the United States.

Other Creeks persisted in learning not only the American political, but the economic, system as well. Although Tallahasseean Lewis Perryman died in a Kansas Civil War refugee camp, his brother George B. Perryman returned to build a business empire based on ranching. In 1868 he married, and the children from this union actively participated in building modern Tulsa.

Government was not the only area of Creek society where whites had a major impact. Missionaries, since removal, had lived among the Five Civilized Tribes and thereby had been available to Indians and their black slaves for religious or educational instruction. Dedicated, yet often ethnocentric, the young men and women of the cloth were filled with dreams of saving souls and were determined to spread the bounties of Western Civilization. These proselytizers finally established a mission school, in the Creek Nation, of which some Tallahasseeans took advantage, although the first educational institution located in the town would not exist until the early 1880s.

At first the Creeks were not receptive to Christianity because they tended to resent white strangers. Sister Mary Agnes Newchurch, one of the first Catholic missionaries to the Creek Nation, recalled that "the older Indians did not like the sisters or even religion." For years, before and after the Civil War, all denominations suffered. Bishop Theophile Meerschaert recounted that Creek antagonism marred the opening of the Catholic Church at Eufaula, Indian Territory. Such resistance dampened the spirits of many, and a good number of the preachers returned home to easily salvageable souls. A few remained and quietly resolved to work harder at their burden.

The first Presbyterian missionary to experience noticeable success in the Creek Nation was Reverend Robert M. Loughridge. In 1841 the Presbyterian Board of Home Missions dispatched Rev-

Tallahassee schoolchildren (not registered), 1880. (*Courtesy of the Thomas Gilcrease Institute of American History and Art, Tulsa, Oklahoma*)

erend Loughridge to the area. Although others had come before him, Loughridge found that they had done more harm than good. None had established friendly rapport with the natives, and tribal officials expelled many who offended the locals with their condescending behavior. After considerable bargaining, the Creeks tentatively agreed to allow Loughridge tenure, but on condition that he preach only at one of the old mission stations built years earlier. The Indians also insisted that Loughridge and his future assistants not interfere with Creek government affairs. In return, the Indians promised to support the project and allot pasture for cattle and foodstuffs to church personnel.

Loughridge and six assistants selected a location at Coweta, Indian Territory. In 1847 he found a more favorable site twelve miles from Fort Gibson, also in Indian Territory. By this time the Creeks were well established in their surroundings and were prepared to assume responsibility for a mission school under the new treaty of 1845, which promised that the United States would appropriate annually $3,000 for educating Creek children. Indians consented with the understanding that the United States Government,

Students at Tulsa's Presbyterian Mission School, built in 1884, located at southeast corner of Fourth and Boston. (*Courtesy of the Beryl Ford Collection, Tulsa, Oklahoma*)

the Creek Nation, and the Board of Home Missions split expenses. The Creeks retained a voice in the day-to-day operation by insisting that they had the right to choose a board of trustees to work with the Presbyterian Superintendent of Public Instruction for the Nation.

The school was named none other than "Tallahassee," and construction began in 1848 under Loughridge's supervision. Once completed it became the white socialization center of learning for the Creek people. The main building stood three stories high. The superintendent and his family lived in the south wing, which was separated from the north part of the building by a spacious hall and dining room in which everyone ate meals. Male and female students were segregated at all times. The girls lived in quarters on the third floor of the north wing in the main building; the boys occupied third-floor rooms in the south wing. Visitation by the opposite sex inside the living quarters was forbidden, and classrooms were on the second floor.

The school officially opened on January 1, 1850 with William Schenck Robertson as the first principal and head teacher. Unfortunately, neither he nor the other teachers knew the Creek language, so students who spoke both tongues served as interpreters. During the first eight years the curriculum consisted of courses in reading, arithmetic, geography, English grammar, and composition. By 1858 spelling, writing, algebra, natural philosophy, history, declamation, and Latin broadened the offerings. These activities occupied six hours a day, with two or three hours of nightly homework.

The school operated under a manual labor plan. Not only were students required to work hard in the classrooms, but they also handled certain jobs around the mission. Girls laundered and mended clothes and helped prepare meals; during the season they also assisted in canning fruits picked from the orchard. Boys worked on the small farm, cultivated the garden, and chopped firewood. Such activities were common in boarding schools, as administrators believed (as the Puritans had) that "an idle mind was the devil's playground."

Despite a four-year interruption during the Civil War, the institution continued to expand into a major school within the Creek Nation and as a successful Christianizing influence. Moses Perryman, of Tulsa, pursued his studies there and later served as a Presbyterian minister; and Principal Robertson's daughter Alice, who became the first Oklahoma Congresswoman (in 1920), attended the Tallahassee school. At no time did it have more than eighty-one students, but its contribution to education in the Creek Nation was immeasurable. Young children who labored long and hard gained insights into white society that served well the Creek Nation in the years that followed.

Thus, before the surge of whites began filtering into Tallahassee during the 1870s, a generation of townspeople was exposed to, and changed by, white society. Creeks had adopted a system of government patterned after that of the United States, and missionaries, dedicated to spreading Christianity and a knowledge of Western civilization, invaded the Creek mind. As always, change taught some Tallahasseeans to thrive in a new environment and forced others to live forever alienated from ancestral ways.

II

Cowtown Tulsa

Throughout the remaining decades of the nineteenth century, industrialization's impact reverberated in Tallahassee and transformed it into cowtown Tulsa. Ranchers, cattle trailers, railroad men, and farmers converged on Indian Territory and created a situation that left Creeks little choice–acculturate again or perish.

While Christian missionaries and the United States government infiltrated Creek society, by the mid-1860s the ranching industry began preparing Tallahassee for modernization and the twentieth century. "Lochapoka Crossing," located near the town, was one of the first heavily used routes that began in southeast Texas and ended in Kansas. Although herders eventually abandoned it for more well-defined roads east and west of town, the Texas cattlemen, whose beef meatpackers made routes available to the North and South, relentlessly drove thousands of animals across the Creek Nation. Paradoxically, drovers discovered and broadened the same paths that Indians had cut to reach Great Plains buffalo and trading posts. These inroads soon became highways for the epoch drives that characterized the post-Civil War American West, but the process disrupted Indian life, trampled crops, and scattered game like deer and elk. Suffering also, Tallahassee livestock often contracted the disease "Texas fever" from the nomadic herds. Seemingly unconcerned with such problems, cowboys and cattle obediently continued to trudge to market.

Abandoned by Mexican settlers during the Texas Revolution in 1836, longhorns had roamed the open prairie for decades. With no natural enemies and plenty of nourishment, the species procreated at an astonishing rate, thereby providing a ready supply of food. During the immediate postwar era, Texans rounded up unbranded mavericks and pushed them north toward railroad terminals in Abilene and Dodge City, Kansas. The scavenger approach soon gave way to more lucrative large-scale operations. Sellers reaped enormous profits, for a mature animal that sold for six dollars in Texas was worth ten times that in the north.

Tallahassee was a favorite stop for the trail bosses and cowhands, who dubbed the area "Tulsi." Cattle always lost weight on the long trips, but land surrounding the hamlet fattened and watered them on buffalo or bluestem grass mixed with sage and added to abundant brooks, streams, and rivers. Rolling hills, blanketed in varying shades of green and set against pale-blue sky, presented a picturesque site for a man to posture himself majestically upon the land that soon would be his. The conqueror's life was not always plush, however, for weather, rustlers, and sickness plagued the excursions. Despite the Tallahassee respite, therefore, a herd often straggled into the railheads.

While some townspeople felt like helpless pawns merely standing in the way of progress, others carefully scrutinized their enemy for weaknesses and discovered a way to survive and benefit from the new era. Traditionally the tribe charged specific families with farming communally-owned Creek land. After removal some Indians took or bought personal control of large tracts in the new Creek Nation. John Severs was one such individual who reasoned that he and even the Nation could charge for grazing rights, netting increased revenue for all concerned. Severs speculated that the venture might also thwart antagonisms between the Creek Nation and the cattle-trailing industry. His idea appealed to others, and by the late 1870s Texas men drove thousands of animals to Tallahassee's outlying areas. Arriving in late spring or early summer, many drives remained throughout the warm months; then, in the fall, cowhands organized roundups and pushed the cattle north. When railroads began operating in and around the town, the procedure proved more successful because beef on the hoof was then shipped for open-range feeding to other nearby points.

Josiah Perryman, Tulsa's first postmaster. (*Courtesy of the Beryl Ford Collection, Tulsa, Oklahoma*)

Even low-quality mixed and scrub cattle prospered in the agreeable climate along the Arkansas River, and soon Texans and Tallahasseeans formed mutually profitable business alliances. Although Severs's innovation did show some ambitious Creeks that individual enterprise could produce wealth and comfort, it also helped kill communal Creek ways.

Heightened activity around "Tulsi" spurred the United States Postal Service to open the Tulsa Station, in 1879, located three and one-half miles north of town on the ranch of George B. Perryman, a politically powerful and wealthy mixed-blood Creek. Although some Creeks did not accept the new spelling and pronunciation, the change soon became a part of the average citizen's lexicon. Many residents were quite eager about the prospect of communicating with old friends and family, but the outpost seldom was busy. Sometimes months passed between letters, and service was slow until the railroad would provide a better, faster carrier.

Osage Indians with white friends on Main Street of Tulsa, Indian Territory, 1893. (*Courtesy of the Beryl Ford Collection, Tulsa, Oklahoma*)

General prosperity from the livestock trade began attracting more Anglos from outside the Nation. In 1881 Bill Jackson became the first white man and Texas rancher to settle around the town when he leased the huge Spike S. Ranch. Within a year he controlled a herd numbering 12,000. Harry C. Hull, an early migrant railroad entrepreneur, made an agreement, which others soon copied, with several Indian farmers. Hull and his associates fenced a large acreage of land (at a site near the present West First Street) and charged a rental fee. The partners shared equally in the profits and received a handsome annual return on their investment for many years to come.

Penning cattle added another dimension to the booming frontier settlement and helped Kansas City and Chicago buyers escape an unmerciful, unpredictable market. If the demand for beef dropped, the sellers refused to sell their inventory until prices rose

Aunt Rachel (as old woman), wife of George Perryman, on porch of her home near Thirty-eighth and Trenton, Tulsa, Oklahoma. (*Courtesy of the Beryl Ford Collection, Tulsa, Oklahoma*)

to a more acceptable level. Creeks living around Tulsa rapidly increased the sizes of their herds, adding to the volume of business. Perryman doubled his personal fortune between 1881 and 1894 by renting thousands of acres south of town from the Creek Nation; there he raised one of the largest herds in the Indian Territory. In 1883, cattle in Texas cost $.75 each and sold for $15.50 a head in Kansas City; therefore, men such as W. E. Halsell, an Owasso, Kansas rancher later instrumental in bringing the Frisco Railroad to Tulsa, expected to generate ten times their initial investments. With opportunities such as these, few could resist the Tulsa lure.

James Monroe Daugherty, of Denton, Texas, was no exception. In 1866, when less than twenty years of age, he helped drive 500 yearlings from South Texas to Kansas and Missouri. In returning home Daugherty hired four cowboys at $40.00 a month, promising to pay them from future dividends; after buying provisions for the trip, also on credit, he had only $1.15 in his pocket. In Abilene, Kansas he sold many of the animals for more than 200 percent profit. In the next several years he returned many times, always with the same results. Nineteen years later he leased a ranch from Legus Perryman, George's brother, for one-half cent an acre, and by 1890 he was pasturing 22,000 head of cattle for Texas ranchers. Within six years he had doubled his operating capacity and retired one of the most wealthy men in the Creek Nation. Daugherty was not the only one who enjoyed prodigious wealth; Arthur J. Smith and William E. Gentry soon joined him. While both in their late twenties, in 1879, the pair emigrated to Tulsa, searching employment. Within a few months they contracted the use of Creek farms, and twenty years later they had made a fortune buying and selling cattle transported from Texas.

Towns that booming industries engulf are generally characterized by haphazard organization, and Tulsa was no exception. Traveler Lilah D. Lindsey, a teacher from Highland Institute in Hillsboro, Ohio, described the settlement as a chaotic place in which "cattle, horses, cows, and pigs roamed the streets at will" and "people sat on their front steps, ate their watermelons, and threw the rinds to . . . obliging pigs." Moreover, former territorial missionary Eliza Moffitt, while addressing a church crowd in Boston, Massachusetts, described Tulsa as "a wasteland."

The stockmen were the first to institute some kind of order and discipline, at least within the practice of their own trade. By the fall of 1884 Creek and white ranchers organized a livestock association and divided the town's immediate area into two districts separated by the Arkansas River. Various men had responsibility for patrolling for rustlers, gathering strays, and organizing roundups in the spring. The membership elected Chief Pleasant Porter as the first president, and Daniel Childres served as the inspector at Tulsa and Catoosa, Indian Territory, the locations at which owners assembled their beef. Childres judiciously checked each brand when cowboys crowded herds into the loading pens. The association paid him five dollars a month for his work, and at the time of his death he could identify more than 100 brands.

The early cattle trails, which had brought prosperity to Tulsa, began to give way to railroads. Early in the 1880s, railroad companies began laying track into the Creek Nation. Ranchers welcomed the innovation, which eventually eliminated the need for trailing. Ironically, the new mechanized transportation had in the 1860s given life to the cattle-trailing industry but just as quickly ended it two decades later. Tulsa business people, similar to their colleagues in cities from St. Louis, Missouri, to San Francisco, California, or from Galveston, Texas, to Abilene, Kansas, were pleased, because modernization brought urban commercial growth. The "iron horse," however, symbolized many things to different people. As author Frank Norris later explained in *The Octopus,* to thriving capitalists it was the outstretched hand, the artery through which the blood of industrialization flowed; yet, Norris explained, to many farmers it brought monopoly, fixed freight rates, and economic devastation. To unassimilated Indians it was another harbinger of white technological superiority, which brought destruction of the buffalo and invaded cherished lands.

In August 1882 the Frisco, then known as the Atlantic and Pacific, was the first line to reach Tulsa. Seven years earlier the company had constructed track from Pierce, Missouri, to Vinita, Indian Territory. Not satisfied with the volume of business, the owners were seeking a new terminal when they sold the enterprise to the Frisco Railroad in January of 1882. Within a matter of days the new operators had a contract to extend the line from Vinita to a point southwest on the Arkansas River, just inside

Cherokee Nation, Indian Territory. Frisco manager Harry Hall knew Cherokee laws prohibited all whites, except those naturalized through intermarriage, from trading inside its borders. Under the more liberal Creek statutes, however, anyone could negotiate deals with a citizen, provided he filed a $10,000 bond with the United States Secretary of the Interior and paid taxes on any merchandise he exported from the jurisdiction. No commercial location could exceed two acres of land, and all money-making ventures required permits. After weighing the facts, contractors Major Clarence B. Gunn of Kansas City, Missouri, Charles M. Condon, and Harry C. Hall, both of Oswego, Kansas, and B. F. Hobart of St. Louis opted to move the terminus inside the Creek domain, 100 yards from the Tulsa city limits.

Gunn, as engineer, oversaw construction and subcontracting, while Hall controlled the finances, made out the payroll, bought supplies, and operated the general undertaking of railroad construction. Condon and Hobart were the financiers and made final decisions on all prospective arrangements. James M. Hall, Harry's brother, was in charge of the company store, which moved with each extension of the line.

When workers finished grading and positioning tracks as far as Catoosa, construction halted for two months until many Tulsa citizens joined the railroad gang and constructed a bridge across the Verdigris and Arkansas rivers. Camps of subcontractors continued to advance along the right-of-way, surveying the land. In early July the Hall brothers pitched the company-store tent on the north side of the right-of-way between present Main Street and Boston Avenue. Indian chiefs, cowmen, and now railroad barons molded Tulsa, and for their role history designated the Halls founders of modern Tulsa.

On August 1, 1882 the construction wagon, loaded with laborers and supplies, arrived from Catoosa, and work began on the terminal located between Tulsa's present-day streets Boston and Main. The crew passed the night in rancher Chauncy A. Owen's boarding tent, which also served as headquarters until completion of the tracks in mid-August. The finished product, which later became Union Station, consisted of a two-stall roundhouse and a section house. Owen moved his establishment north of the terminus, and workers built stockyards, with loading pens and chutes, south of the tracks.

The first train arrived on the morning of August 21, and soon a mixed bag of customers and cargo made regular trips to Vinita. The fare was five cents a mile, and James Hall recalled that the ride was leisurely; he noted that the only connection was with the passenger line to St. Louis, so there was ample time for travelers and crew to shoot prairie chickens along the way. Boxcars full of cattle constantly journeyed east. In fact the *Indian Journal*, a Muskogee newspaper, described Tulsa and the neighboring Red Fork district as the largest shipping points in the territory. In June 1884 more than 150 carloads of "cornfeds" rode to Pauls Valley, Indian Territory, and other towns or embarked daily for Kansas, Missouri, and beyond. In a single day George Perryman once shipped more than five railroad cars of beef from Tulsa to St. Louis. The massive volume of trade continued until the end of the grazing season, in early fall, and even then Tulsans continued to receive and send a steady supply of goods.

Tulsa remained the railroad's farthest point into the Five Civilized Tribes' domain for approximately two years; then a spur line was extended to Red Fork. From there tracks later extended to Sapulpa and Oklahoma City, Indian Territory, and then on to Texas. Prosperity continued with each development, laying a foundation for the future, when oil would be discovered and Oklahoma would become a state. The extensions, however, did not produce competition, for the Frisco alone serviced Tulsa for twenty years.

Tulsa's new connection with the outside world invited more wanderers to make the site their home. During the mid-1880s, a collection of Texas, Kansas, Missouri, and Cherokee and Creek Nation seekers joined mixed-bloods, a few former slaves, a cadre of ranchers such as Jackson, and several railroad employee families. From 1,000 to 1,500 people occupied the nascent city throughout the next decade, and many of them would soon become heirs to the financial rewards of a turn-of-the-century economic boom.

During the winter of 1882 Owen replaced his tent with a frame building and christened it "Tulsa House," the only hotel in town. The first general store belonged to Thomas Jefferson Archer, a young mixed-blood Cherokee, who set up shop in March of 1883.

James Monroe Hall, a commissar's agent with the Frisco Railroad, was in Tulsa in the early days with his brother H. C. Hall. He was first a merchant, then a banker and investor, for more than half a century. He is considered by many as the "father" of Tulsa. (*Courtesy of the Beryl Ford Collection, Tulsa, Oklahoma*)

Harry C. Hall, founder of Tulsa. (*Courtesy of the Beryl Ford Collection, Tulsa, Oklahoma*)

Harry Hall decided to be the competition, in April of that year, when he and brother James opened another mercantile. Soon the Perryman brothers transferred their store from Red Fork to Tulsa. Each of these establishments employed two full-time clerks and advertised "a complete full line of groceries, dry goods, and farm implements." By the late spring of 1883 the community had two physicians, a drugstore, and a lumber yard.

In 1882, also, John R. Broady began printing the *Tulsa World*, a newspaper that generally supported Republican Party positions. The tabloid's stance was quite understandable when one considered that a Republican-dominated federal government made political-patronage appointments, such as marshals, Indian agents, and military personnel, throughout much of the 1880s and '90s.

Social life matched the burgeoning economy. Few families and

Thomas Jefferson Archer, early Tulsa merchant. Archer was killed in 1894 when explosives were set off accidentally in his general merchandise store. (*Courtesy of the Beryl Ford Collection, Tulsa, Oklahoma*)

Chauncey Owen established Tulsa's first boarding tent on Main Street in 1893 and later built Tulsa's first hotel, called "Tulsa House." (*Courtesy of the Beryl Ford Collection, Tulsa, Oklahoma*)

none of the emerging social clubs missed an opportunity to organize an event. Dances, held periodically in someone's home or at Heney Grove, on the outskirts of town, were the most popular entertainment. Here women wore their best dresses and arranged their hair in a stylish fashion, while scores of men outfitted themselves in probably the one good suit they owned. Couples whirled around the floor until well after midnight, while onlookers prattled enthusiastically. Such occasions did a great deal to engender a feeling of belonging and to promote courtship or marriage, all essential components of a society. On a more regular basis, residents gathered wherever they could find a place to visit; E. B. Harris remembered men clustered around his father's store, whiling away the time telling exaggerated stories and sharing jokes.

Horse races also attracted large, festive audiences. There men

J. M. Hall General Merchandise Store, located on west side of Main Street, Tulsa, Indian Territory, 1894. (*Courtesy of the Beryl Ford Collection, Tulsa, Oklahoma*)

George Perryman house, near today's Thirty-eighth Street and south Trenton Avenue. The house was officially designated the Tulsa Indian Territory Post Office March 25th, 1879; postmaster was George's brother Josiah Perryman. (*Courtesy of the Beryl Ford Collection, Tulsa, Oklahoma*)

watched their quarterhorse ponies, normally used for cutting or roping cattle, create a frenzy of pounding hooves and wild cheers. Cowboys lived by the speed of their horses, for it took quick animals to catch a yearling calf and nimbleness to separate a young bull from the remainder of the herd. A person might brag for months, before a contest, that he had the fastest steed in the territory. Egos took control, and onlookers or participants alike often lost or won several weeks' wages within a few seconds.

Tulsans spent quieter times fishing and hunting. The wooded hills abounded with deer, elk, wild pigeons, turkeys, quail, prairie chickens, and mink. The streams supplied plenty of catfish, trout, and bass, and many people boasted of being expert hunters or fishermen.

In 1880 Tulsa Creeks, determined to prepare their children to cope with a new environment, established the first-recorded neighborhood school, which apparently excluded white students; pupils from the town's emerging center of black residency, the Greenwood District, were also uninvited. The facility accommodated thirty young people, only one of whom could speak English. In 1883 a stealthy man, attesting to be a teacher, collected funds from some local whites who wanted a school for their children, but he promptly took the money and spent it in a local gambling tent. Thus the residents appealed to the Presbyterian Board of Home Missions, and in the fall of 1884 the Creek national government granted missionaries permission to erect, just south of town, a one-room, wooden structure named the Presbyterian Mission School. Serving both Indians and whites, the building rested on what is today the southeast corner of Fourth Street and Boston Avenue, and throughout the decades both City Hall and a Board of Education edifice have occupied the same spot.

The church sent Reverend W. P. Haworth, currently preaching in Vinita, to become pastor of the mission's church-related work. Mrs. S. J. Stonecipher, of Oswego, Kansas, became the superintendent of educational activities; and Ida Stephens, of Vinita, Indian Territory, took the first instructor's position. Before the general stores carried necessary supplies, dedicated teachers provided all the learning tools for approximately seventy Indian and white pupils whom the school served. Bilingual Creek youngsters volunteered as interpreters, and all the students aided in maintenance of the

Looking north on Main Street near First Street, Tulsa, 1897. (*Courtesy of the Beryl Ford Collection, Tulsa, Oklahoma*)

building and grounds. The Presbyterians struggled financially, however, to keep their classes going just nine months out of every twelve; even a tuition and fixed teacher salary of thirty dollars a month eventually would prove inadequate to sustain the concern for more than fourteen years, although it did lay the groundwork for Tulsa's first public education system.

In addition to the mission school, Reverend Haworth assumed responsibility for the First Presbyterian Church, which in 1882 began congregating regularly in a large tent. Agnes Slater, wife of a local carpenter, was the first superintendent. Although she was a Congregationalist, Slater and a Baptist preacher, William P. Booker, organized the Union Sunday School, appropriately named for a flock composed of no fewer than eight different faiths. When Reverend Haworth arrived, in 1884, he began holding services in the Presbyterian mission and ministered to the group for fifteen years.

Soon the First Methodist Episcopal Church built its own facility at North Main and Brady, and in the fall of 1888 Pastor George W. Mowbray's sisters, Mattie and Anna, opened a school for underprivileged children. In 1895 another institution emerged under the auspices of the Methodist Episcopal Church South; both were located north of the railroad, near Boulder Avenue, and, like all the other religious-centered day schools, this last one survived until 1899.

A need other than the desire to reform or educate the young brought men and women to church and school activities. Participants always lingered after services, engaging in conversation filled with laughter, back-slapping, and warm feelings. Church socials never lacked attendance, for everyone shared food and drink and enjoyed a peaceful Sunday afternoon. The quest for companionship also manifested itself in the founding of a fraternal order. On August 8, 1893, eleven men organized the Ancient Free and Accepted Masons of Tulsa, Lodge Number Sixty-five. Philander Reeder was the first Worshipful Master, and the Masonic Lodge enlisted top civic figures for years.

A crime wave unfortunately was another repercussion of Tulsa's expansion. The disruption of security antagonized segregationist Creeks and gave the ambitious an excellent case for arguing that the federal government should convince the Five Civilized Tribes to repeal restrictions and open up their land to the "civilizing"

Jim Daugherty cowboys on ranch east of Tulsa, 1898. (*Courtesy of the Beryl Ford Collection, Tulsa, Oklahoma*)

Typical ranch chuck wagon. (*Courtesy of the Beryl Ford Collection, Tulsa, Oklahoma*)

Ferry and cattle drive crossing the Arkansas River near today's Eleventh Street bridge, 1895. (*Courtesy of the Beryl Ford Collection, Tulsa, Oklahoma*)

influence of white family settlers. Cattlemen worked and played hard, and they spent many Saturday nights drinking, gambling, and cavorting until the early morning hours. Ranching baron Joseph G. McCoy vividly recalled in his memoirs that drunken cowboys often rode through the streets, firing guns and screaming. When ranch hands were not terrorizing the locals, gangs of cutthroats roamed freely, and law-abiding persons either remained at home after dark or carried guns for protection. Men with mysterious pasts and names such as "Texas Jack," "Cherokee Bill," or "Yockey" were familiar and fearful fixtures in Hall Brothers' or Owen's boarding houses. They infested the Indian Territory with robbery or rustling and found hideouts near Tulsa. The famous Dalton brothers–Grant, Bob, and Emmett–lived in town most of their lives. Safes of local merchants were thieves' easy prey, for the settlement had no bank until 1885, and the sheriff's job was often vacant.

Peace officers enforced Arkansas, Kansas, and Texas laws more strictly than did Indian Territory officials enforce local laws, so Tulsans attempted to observe a "gentlemen's agreement" with prospective marauders–to offer asylum in return for protection; therefore, the Dalton, Glass, and Cook families rarely harassed the locals. Unfortunately such an understanding was doomed, because cattle rustling was the major problem, and no rancher could afford to have his stock pilfered. The animals often strayed into Cherokee Territory in which unscrupulous men considered them fair game.

As stealing became more predominant, Tulsans put up rewards for information leading to a wanted person's apprehension. Vigilante committees were common–but not always productive. Shawnee Hardridge, Tulsa's first policeman, once had the ignoble misfortune of drafting men to help track two horse thieves, only to have his deputies desert when gunfire began. Hoping to avoid a repetition, Hardridge thereafter offered immediate rewards for citizen assistance. James Hall recalled helping track the Glass coterie, which terrorized eastern Kansas and the Indian Territory. Tulsans and outlaws clashed outside the town's limits, and although the villains escaped, authorities captured a collection of stolen horses and a wagon loaded with illegal whiskey. To compensate for losing the prey, Hardridge impounded the liquor, and his deputies "had a sustained drunk."

Clifford Goldsby, "Cherokee Bill," at age fourteen, a notorious Indian Territory outlaw who was hanged in Fort Smith, Arkansas, at age twenty. (*Courtesy of the Beryl Ford Collection, Tulsa, Oklahoma*)

Hunters Christmans display of local game in front of the Wallace & Calhoun Meat Market, located on the east side of Main between First and Second streets, 1896. (*Courtesy of the Beryl Ford Collection, Tulsa, Oklahoma*)

Once apprehended, lawbreakers usually faced swift justice, and rarely did a defendant go unpunished. Federal Judge Isaac Parker, at Fort Smith, Arkansas, well earned his nickname, "the hanging judge," and others who served on the bench followed a similar philosophy. If acquitted of one charge, alleged criminals might find themselves confronted with other fabricated accusations. Once, when a Tulsa jury found a black man innocent of horse stealing, the magistrate countered, "If the Negro didn't steal that horse, I know one he did, [so let's] hang him anyway." Such unorthodox justice symbolized law and order in Tulsa and throughout the Indian Territory.

United States marshals were headquartered at Fort Smith, 100 miles to the southeast, but their jurisdiction covered all of Indian Territory, an area too large to police adequately. Because of the vast, open space, too much time usually elapsed between the act and arrest, and all too often the fugitive stayed one step ahead of his tracker. Before entering Tulsa, hoodlums climbed surrounding hills and studied hitchracks through field glasses to be certain that their pursuers were not in town. Enforcers therefore sometimes ambushed their quarry, as opposed to taking them live. In Tulsa, such was the Dalton and the Doolin gangs' fate. Naturally, the desperadoes retaliated by making, on unsuspecting citizens, nightly raids that ended in gunplay and death.

Logistics hampered individuals in reporting crimes. If someone wanted to inform federal authorities of wrongdoing, he or she boarded a train to Monet, Missouri, and switched to another bound for Fort Smith. The alternative route required a four-day trip overland by horseback. Both excursions took time and money and were filled with the ever-present expectation of retaliation. Thus law-abiding townspeople interested in civic development organized to lobby for better protection.

No doubt the Creek element was divided on the issue. Although it eschewed the havoc wreaked on all honest people, many Indians accustomed to negotiating with the federal government realized that better law enforcement meant more white domination. The *Indian Journal* nevertheless crusaded for an end to the turbulence, noting that local officers were often as bad as the crooks or were noted for their incompetency rather than for devotion to duty. Believing that the Creek Nation and United States governments would never adequately combine forces to protect Indian Territorial citizens, whites joined some Indians who demanded that the Creek Nation be admitted into the Union as a territory. Gradually the federal government became blind to its current treaties that allowed tribes self-governing rights and instead heard only the annexation cries.

Traditional Creeks easily recognized that they were losing control of what was once their village. In a vain effort to check the social changes incurred from new capitalist concerns, early in the 1880s the Creek General Council passed a series of laws specifying the conditions under which a non-citizen might enter the Nation and the length of time he might stay within its borders. The tribe precluded any who married Creeks from becoming citizens, although the mixed-blood offspring continued to unite with the tribe. The Indians further discouraged migration by legally defining all new arrivals as "sojourners" and subjecting them to threats of removal for minor offenses. The Council also came to grips with the controversial practice of Creeks' engaging white employees, thereby pitting assimilated Creeks against conservative ones. Some had taken up the custom after the Civil War and had since adamantly supported the move as an economic necessity; however, increasing tensions within the tribe pressured the leaders to conclude that, although the new custom could continue, all employers were to pay a "head tax" for the right. Purebloods made certain that the ordinance was conscientiously enforced and that violators paid heavy fines.

Creeks remained divided over the residency issue. Such friction worked, as it had done throughout the century, to weaken what could have been a united Indian position. Those who saw profit in "civilizing" never convinced stalwarts that adaptation to the white culture was an inevitable step toward personal success. Conservatives, however, refused to define survival in terms of individual profit, and by the century's end they became Tulsa's disinherited.

Immigrants habitually violated the anti-white Creek statutes, and chaos, which was the product of Indian and United States representatives' inability or recalcitrance to coordinate policies, protected intruders. Indian Territory's dual judicial system, composed of Creek Nation and United States courts, was part of the 1866 treaties. The bodies therefore often battled over the concept of justice and legal jurisdictions, with few peaceful and satisfactory results. Moreover, federal justices sometimes merely aggravated potentially hostile disputes by brandishing their power to activate the United States cavalry that was stationed at Fort Smith. In addition, Indian agents were supposed to regulate interaction between the two societies, but the men were notoriously lax. Many were unqualified or were more interested in embezzling funds than in fairly enforcing their orders; however, some were well meaning individuals whom Creek distrust rendered powerless.

In a last-ditch effort to loosen the Anglo-oriented grasp on destiny, some militant Creeks initiated the Green Peach War in 1883. Their aim was to drive pioneers out of Tulsa, but federal troops handily defeated the outnumbered band. In 1887 Congress passed the Dawes Act, which forced all the first Americans to accept Anglo laws and made them wards of the United States government. Politicians determined that the western half of antebellum Indian Territory, which became a reservation for Plains Indians and other rebellious tribes after the Civil War, would now be Oklahoma Territory.

The twin territories were suddenly open for settlement, and wagons by the thousands from every part of the United States passed through Tulsa. In 1893 people felt the stirring of a mighty movement when the Cherokee Outlet was opened to white settlement, and, in a series of dramatic "runs" beginning in 1889, hordes of United States citizens scrambled to possess the coveted land. The Cherokee Nation was no more, and the last generation of Creeks to ever be a part of an autonomous Indian Nation stood poised to hear a pistol's fire and watch the end of its civilization be gobbled up under horses' hooves.

The same year that the Cherokee Run occurred, officials of the United States government appointed a Dawes Commission to close out the affairs of the Cherokees, the Creeks, and other tribes living in eastern Oklahoma. These federal agents possessed the power to divide Indian lands into 160-acre tracts and allot the surveyed strips to individuals currently farming the plots either for personal gain or under the collective control system. Theoretically only Creeks were entitled to the land; however, in order to keep property, Indians had to prove that they were eligible. The commission registered names on tribal rolls, and only those listed received allotments. If an occupant did not make his or her claim within sixty days it was sold at public auction, at the low price of $1.25 an acre. Revenue from the sale was used in a futile attempt to compensate the Creek Nation for all territory lost to whites since its dealings with them began.

Incensed by Washington's overt destruction of Indian tradition and law, the Creeks refused to submit without a legal fight. They argued that if the United States government intended to enforce what the Creeks considered an insidious statute, then the Indians were no longer self-governing but were subject to United States legislation without the protection of being American citizens. Not since the end of slavery had a minority group of people been maneuvered into such an impotent position. A bitter irony was that many slave-holding Creeks had during Reconstruction willingly supported the annihilation of the Fourteenth and Fifteenth Amendment rights to which freedmen were constitutionally entitled; yet Indian bigotry had all been a part of the acculturation scenario that progressive Creeks envisioned since before removal. Instead of being accepted by the dominant society members, the Indians, like the blacks, acquired institutional racism in exchange for much of their land and their entire way of life. Creek attorneys appealed for justice and humane treatment, using documented arguments, historical facts, and legal precedents to support their points; but federal judges were unmoved. Courts held that any town within Indian Territory had the right to incorporate under existing statutes. The decision ended Creek hope for victory, and the tribe grudgingly submitted to the Dawes Commission.

Other Tulsans welcomed the news with wild rejoicing, for it meant that "progress" was on the way. By 1897 there were in the town thirty-eight business firms operating under traders' licenses. In addition, numerous illegal "intruders" who had formerly held no right to prosper within the Creek Nation soon obtained lawful status. These new Tulsa civic leaders wasted no time in presenting a petition of incorporation to a United States court, which approved the measure on January 18, 1898.

The next step was to buy city property from the Creeks. The Curtis Act, passed the same year that Tulsa incorporated, outlined the procedure for sectioning the site and stipulated how occupants could receive large concessions from selling renovated acreages. Implementing the new policy unearthed many problems. Although the white-educated Indians were familiar with federal laws, none of them, before now, had ever been forced to live solely under United States rule. Consequently Creeks were uncertain as to what constituted legal ownership or use of land. For years the Dawes Commission received a stream of letters stressing both the extreme hardships from which Creeks suffered and the dire need for help in explaining an alien political and economic system.

When the Dawes Commission divided and distributed land to individuals, many Indians could not make the adjustment to a new capitalistic life style. Further difficulties resulted from federal government delays in pairing a family with a small tract of land, which may have been part of a larger chunk farmed as Creek communal property. Thus acres of earth either faltered into a state of disrepair or fell into the grasp of some more aggressive Indians.

Commissioners also required tribal citizens to state their claims in person before a federal judge or a civilian authorized to take petitions. The time and expense involved in traveling on the frontier proved to be a severe hardship for the prospective farmers, and it was not uncommon for them to wait long hours, perhaps even days, before they received a hearing. The Dawes Act, however, was a final pronouncement, and the Creeks were faced with either complying with its directives or losing what was left of their lands. They therefore stood in line and hoped agents would be fair; yet, even as they waited, white emigrants squatted on and rationalized the theft of holdings that they believed "Americans" were destined to possess.

Hoping to receive easy cash, profiteers entered into lively speculative development by erecting flimsy buildings on which they hastily filed occupancy titles, sometimes under fictitious Indian relatives' names. Overnight fences surrounded grassy fields, and one-room shacks decorated the landscape; some of the more industrious charlatans even plowed strips of ground.

The Commission realized that hustlers were grasping cheap land and reselling it for a better price. To avoid mutilating the Curtis Act's intent, which was to reward legitimate owners' developments, the commissioners determined to appraise lots without regard to the value of improvements and sell them to occupants for a fraction of the property's worth. If the resident did not buy his land, then the government sold it at public auction; however, no matter what price a plot brought, the former holder received only that part of the revenue that did not exceed the low estimated assessment. Finally the commissioners placed the sale money in the United States Treasury on credit for the Creeks. Ingenious individuals or "lot jumpers" devised plans for either purchasing land at a discount or else making an extremely profitable sale. Although they were not well liked in the community, no one was able or willing to rout them out. Some fairly honorable whites who wanted to encourage population growth believed the best way to achieve success was to liberalize the Dawes Commission policies. To control the skulduggery, federal agents also attempted to prevent Creeks from selling their land for a number of years. The Indians, however, considered the proposed protection an insinuation that whites were superior business people, capable of outsmarting the slow-witted red man. Although the government lifted the restriction, it always retained the right to approve all transactions.

In addition to its other duties, the Dawes Act administration employed a surveyor named J. Gus Patton and his brother Dan to organize Tulsa for future growth. The Pattons used the Frisco track as their base line and accepted the old designation for Main Street. The pair named roads west of and parallel to Main after western American cities and dubbed streets east of Main after eastern metropolises. When they were finished, in December of 1901, the Pattons had created a 654.58-acre plot from what had formerly been Creek Tulsa's location and had formed a local government that operated as an adjunct of the Dawes Commission. Rather than accept an open-market value, the surveyors fixed the site's value at $1,071.73, an excessively low figure. They expected to entice further migration, but devaluation of the town showed little regard for treating Creeks fairly. The sale, which took place in 1902, generated only $659 for the Creek Nation. Henceforth, tribal leaders sounded a cry of fraud, and for more than fifty years they fought the United States to recover lost revenue from the townsite sale. Despite all the conflict and distrust, some natives reaped handsome sums of money in exchange for their property, although the transactions forever brought an end to any semblance of Creek Tulsa.

Many Creek and white cattlemen had influenced the modernization of Tulsa, which helped them provide food for millions of Americans. Although the livestock trade continued to exist through the Tulsa stockyards, the solitary, rural, economic reign over the town was brief, for the twentieth century made history of cowtown Tulsa. The consciousness of Tulsa and the nation would no longer idolize the yeoman farmer or rancher, and John D. Rockefeller soon would personify the idea of success. Moreover, old Tallahassee's role in America's path to greatness was just beginning. The stage was set for a new wave of settlers and the event that produced a modern city–the discovery of oil.

III

Oil Capital

The first two decades of the twentieth century witnessed the unearthing of oil surrounding Tulsa. The dramatic and rapid manner in which the location subsequently urbanized necessitated city planning and reform activities similar to those conducted in other cities during the nation's Progressive Era; however, we deal with such developments in "Chapter III," because first we must describe the somewhat spectacular sequence of oil discovery events.

There were early evidences of petroleum in Indian Territory. Cherokee Chief John Ross had discovered it in 1859 while manufacturing salt at Grand Saline on Grand River. Other Indians and traveling whites had seen rivulets of oil seeping from cracks in the earth north of Tahlequah at New Spring Place in Going Snake district, Cherokee Nation, and around the modern-day town of Ardmore, Oklahoma. During frontier days, however, it was a source of exasperation, not of wealth. Dark liquid skimmed water holes in northeastern Indian Territory, causing ranchers to bemoan the first signs of its pollution. Not until gasoline engines and high-speed machinery replaced horses and buggies, and people adapted it to modern technology, would Tulsa virtually explode into a modern city. Indians did not prospect except at territorial towns Bartlesville, Muskogee, and Chelsea, where hunting parties often camped and built their night fires by driving a hollow tube into the ground and igniting the escaping gas. On occasion people used oil as a lubricant, although most individuals preferred grease. Coal and firewood served as fuel for manufacturing in the nation, and whale- and coal-oil lamps or candles illuminated homes and businesses.

Petroleum was not without its sensationalist uses, for hacks advertised it as a miraculous "wonder" drug. Enterprising salesmen bottled the dark, slimy liquid and sold it throughout the American West to gullible settlers who dreamed of recapturing their long-departed youthful vitality or whose sufferings were obviously psychosomatic. In his annual report of 1853 the Indian agent reported his naiveté:

> The oil springs in this nation are attracting considerable attention, as they are said to be a remedy for all chronic diseases. Rheumatism stands no chance at all, and the worst cases of dropsy yield to its effects.

Thus, while potential Tulsa area fields lay unexplored, the Texas Spindletop discovery startled the world and began the rabid scramble to the southwest for "black gold."

With the prodigious Texas find, news quickly spread that prospectors could unearth oil in Indian Territory. On November 9, 1899, an independent driller, John S. Wick, subleased (from Chief Lucas Perryman and other prominent Creeks) 410,000 acres of Red Fork, Indian Territory, land located a few miles from Tulsa. The site began at the Arkansas River, ran north to the Frisco Railroad, and extended across the waterway into Oklahoma Territory. Wick had closely examined the geology and concluded that oil was somewhere under the property. Although eager to drill, he was without equipment. He obsessively fantasized, however, about becoming another John D. Rockefeller, so he frantically tried to interest a partner. Wick's incessant prattle finally attracted Jesse A. Heydrick, an experienced Pennsylvanian, and the two men consolidated, with Wick controlling the land and Heydrick furnishing the rigs. Unfortunately, before the workers could begin, the contract terms with Perryman expired. Wick and Heydrick were able to strike another agreement on July 16, 1900. In addition to the original signers it included a Red Fork half-blood Creek, Sue A. Bland, who was married to the town's physician, John C. W. Bland. In the late spring of 1901 Heydrick moved his cable-tool rig to Red Fork but could find no one who would cash his New York draft. Finally John Bland, who seemed to be managing his wife's business interests, cashed it with the stipulation that the prospectors drill the first well on Sue Bland's Red Fork forty-acre tract.

Heydrick and Wick did not know it at the time, but Bland and his good friend and fellow doctor, Fred S. Clinton, were planning to use the first strike in a scheme to place Tulsa on the map. According to Clinton, "We decided on a rational development of the community and state, with oil as the magic lure." Clinton raised the money to pay freight and workers, while Bland convinced the drillers that his wife's property should be the site for the first well. Clinton appealed to Henry H. Adams, the Frisco agent at Red Fork, and borrowed $300 to purchase equipment, pledging that the donor would receive a handsome reward for his trust. With all the preliminary work finished, Heydrick machinery began drilling on May 10, 1901. At first the going was slow, but shortly before midnight on Monday, June 24, 1901, crude shot over the top of the derrick.

The strike came at a most inopportune time. Heydrick was in Pennsylvania reassuring some of his eastern stockholders that their investment was safe; Bland was bedridden, unable to attend to business; Wick was sleeping under the rig; and a young, inexperienced worker, Luther Crossman, was in charge of the drilling. Heydrick had previously warned Wick that in the event of a strike he should shut down the well and keep the find a secret. Wick wired his partner, however, that "Oil is spouting over the top . . .," and the word was out. His message, picked up by listening operators, began a stampede of adventurers to Red Fork.

Bland asked Clinton to accept a power of attorney for Sue Bland and, as the Curtis Act required, to file the strike with the Muskogee, Indian Territory, Creek agent. On June 25, the day after the strike, Clinton, armed with a quart bottle of the oil, climbed into his buggy, went to Tulsa, and boarded the first train for Muskogee. He arrived late that evening at the home of his good friend Dr. F. B. Fite. Together they tested the material by pouring a few drops over wood shavings. After igniting the pile, the physicians watched joyfully as the flame, burning bright and strong, proved that the liquid was authentic.

The following morning Fite took Clinton to meet with Allison Aylesworth, the Dawes Commission secretary. After proper introductions, Clinton explained that he represented Sue Bland and was there to file a homestead allotment on her behalf. Aylesworth agreed to the request, and by four o'clock that afternoon Clinton and Fite were on their way back to Red Fork. They arrived at the well on the morning of June 27, 1901, to a scene of mass confusion. Heydrick had not returned to take charge, and Clinton found that several riggers had taken over. Information about the strike had spread throughout the Tulsa-Red Fork area, and hundreds of people begged for work, while scores merely stood around and stared. Clinton soon took command and restored order to the operation.

Rumors spread that the Red Fork strike was the greatest in the history of the oil business and that the well might produce more than 300 barrels a day.* Heydrick, who returned on June 27, feared otherwise, noting that although the mineral fired "high into the air [it] soon [blew] out," resulting in not more than ten.** Bland and Clinton, however, were elated because their dream "to find oil and let the world know about it . . ." seemed to be coming true. Paul Clinton, Fred's son, telegraphed the news to Guthrie resident Fred Barde, who was a reporter for the *Kansas City Star*. Within two days the information drifted north, and the *Kansas City Times* ran banner headlines, "OIL WELL GUSHER FIFTEEN FEET HIGH."

Heydrick's prediction turned out to be correct, for the yet-to-come Glenn Pool and the Cushing, Oklahoma, deposits, also located near Tulsa, would dwarf the Red Fork reservoir. Bland and Clinton, however, had succeeded because their efforts proved that crude was underfoot, and a plethora of fields surrounding the town soon emerged. One day Tulsans would look back and thank the two enterprising doctors for their daring scheme, which led to the making of Tulsa, "Oil Capital of America."

Two wildcatters, Bob Galbreath and Frank Chesley, also played a significant role in the drama when, as agents for the newly established Tulsa-Creek Oil and Gas Company, they leased the Ida Glenn farm on a hunch that black gold was somewhere under-

*Numerous times throughout the chapter we refer to the term "barrels a day" in calculating the amount of oil produced. To avoid being redundant, we henceforth shall omit "barrels a day" and write only a numerical figure.

**This is an example of the note above.

ground. They began drilling on September 17, 1905, and two months later, on November 22, the experiment uncovered a 1,481-foot-deep lagoon. Relieved of the earth's pressure above, natural gas trapped beneath jettisoned oil far into the sky. The original well and the two additional area wells produced 600 and 2,500, respectively, during the first year, which meant that machinery and men retrieved, loaded, and shipped a total of 1,375,000 gallons of oil to the refineries. It seemed that Tulsa-Creek Oil and Gas Company could not furnish enough supplies to keep up with the steady flow roaring from the pipes. In spite of the shortages, the company sank thirty-five wells during the first year of operation and produced 6,000,000 total barrels, selling for $2 million.

Grand-scale successes invited other exploration at Glenn Pool (named for the farm's owner), and by 1907 there were 125 pump jacks sucking from the ground at a fantastic rate. In August of 1906, however, the field was hit with a series of natural disasters, when weeks of hard rain and striking lightning destroyed tons of tankers full of oil. Even so, net outputs continued to reach unprecedented heights. In February of 1907 seventy-seven companies collectively set a record by selling an average of more than 6,954 barrels. The *Daily Oklahoman*, an Oklahoma City, Oklahoma, newspaper, reported in March that some of the new sites were regurgitating even 200, for several days in a row. On July 2, 1906, a Chicago-based firm, the Tide Water Oil Company, wired one of its Indian Territory agents, David F. Connolly, to investigate the Ida Glenn farm, "and if things looked promising, obtain leases in the surrounding area." Connolly contacted his Tulsa friend D. O. Brown, and then the two hired a covered buggy and rode thirty miles to the Galbreath and Chesley wells. The sites' productivity (1,100) astounded the two men, and they immediately contacted Glenn about leasing other portions of his farm. Connolly offered thirty, but Glenn made a counter proposal of seventy-five dollars an acre, and the men finally closed a deal for $1,200. Neither Connolly nor Brown had the authority, however, to purchase leases, and they reasoned that they would lose their jobs if their company balked because Glenn would probably sue. They knew, though, that time was important. Competitors were on the way, and Glenn, who was no fool, could at any moment increase the price. Connolly and Brown were so convinced that the venture was worth gambling for that they purchased a few leases for themselves.

Three days later the pair bought a contiguous Corbrary farm and began drilling, and in the early morning hours of July 13, 1906, they hit a gusher capable of producing at least 3,000. Connolly hurriedly sent a telegram to Tom Riter, an executive at Tide Water Oil Company, ordering "men and steel tanks as soon as possible." Two dozen laborers and forty-two of the huge containers arrived within a few days, and the work began. Glenn Pool subsequently grew in one year from an 80-acre farm to an 800-acre high-quality oil tract, the world's largest. Even though the price fluctuated from thirty-nine to forty-two cents a barrel,* low by today's standards, at the time it was sufficient to encourage operating in the area. An additional inducement was that the funds were "naturals," meaning that the pressure from gas trapped underground pushed crude through the sunken pipe like a geyser, thus eliminating the need for pumps. So valuable was their property that a few years later Galbreath and Chesley refused to sell it for $3 million. The low overhead made drilling relatively inexpensive, an economic fact that overcompensated for the low market value.

The new commercial activity warmed many Tulsans' hearts. In a letter to his son, real estate agent William E. Campbell wrote that the two pipelines shipping oil from the Tulsa area to refineries either on the Gulf of Mexico or in the North "will have all they can handle." Campbell had a right to be exuberant, for he and his associates owned a few of the most valuable plots. "Some of these," he gleefully reported, "have flowed 2,500 to 3,000 barrels in twenty-four hours;" consequently Glenn Pool leases were astronomically high. One group of owners refused to let their property go for the then large sum of $2,500,000. Land that two years earlier had sold for thirteen dollars an acre no one could now touch for any amount.

Small, independent companies initiated all the early operations primarily because their owners and managers were willing to take risks, whereas major oil companies were reluctant to join the bandwagon for fear of overspeculating on a worthless field. By late 1906, however, the Standard Oil Company was ready to allow its sub-

*Henceforth we shall omit the term "a barrel" from a given price.

sidiary, Prairie Oil and Gas, to build two eight-inch pipelines to Baton Rouge, Louisiana. Officials completed and christened them on August 15, 1906. As Campbell had predicted, there was more than enough to go around, and competing firms were no longer hesitant to construct outlets into the underground black springs. By 1906 the twin territories were temporary leaders in production, and Tulsa, coupled with its sister cities, supplied more than 50 percent of the country's consumed petroleum. In February of 1907 the Texas-based Gulf Company constructed additional outlets from Tulsa extending to the Gulf of Mexico. The corporation's executives had worried since the Texas Spindletop strike that the state's production would someday decline, so they subsequently shifted much of their attention to Glenn Pool. The new connection transported approximately 106,000 barrels a week, and the Gulf Company soon expanded its operations throughout the American South and Southwest.

The well that opened Glenn Pool, October 1905. (*Courtesy of the Beryl Ford Collection, Tulsa, Oklahoma*)

Tulsa–Red Fork well, completed in 1901. (*Courtesy of the Beryl Ford Collection, Tulsa, Oklahoma*)

Texaco was not far behind Gulf; in December of 1907 the former erected a pumping station and storage facility southwest of Tulsa, on the west bank of the Arkansas River. The Associated Producers Company soon augmented the project, paying $17,500 for 160 acres in the northern part of the field, a location that soon produced 1,500. When Associated sold its leases two years later, it had in storage more than 1,100,000 full drums.

Following suit, Standard Oil reaped huge sums from its newly acquired sites. By 1908 both national and local oil concerns were operating at full capacity, when the tract hit its peak of 1,117,440. Tulsa's official recognition as the nation's oil center came in 1908, and Patrick C. Doyle, from Beaumont, Texas, purchased a small weekly publication named *Oil Investors* and transported his presses to Tulsa. Texas retained the oil state title, but the new journal stayed in Oklahoma. Doyle changed the name to *The Oil and Gas Journal* and built it from a weekly pamphlet into what old-timers called the industry's bible. Printed in five languages, its worldwide circulation brought international acclaim to northeastern Oklahoma. Even Tulsa's arch rival, Oklahoma City, grudgingly acknowledged that the former might someday "be the Pittsburgh of the Southwest."

By 1912 investments in 4,986 wells totaled around $11 million

Cimarron ferry crossing, in the oil fields between Drumright and Oilton, Oklahoma. (*Courtesy of the Beryl Ford Collection, Tulsa, Oklahoma*)

in equipment and salaries. Pipeline companies invested another $50 million in underground throughways running from Oklahoma to the Gulf or the Atlantic Ocean. The Tulsa-Creek Oil and Gas Company never failed to pay a stockholder dividend, while other conglomerates doled out monthly royalties up to $15,000 to each of their partners.

The Cushing discovery in 1912, a find that eventually overwhelmed seasoned oil men throughout the world, had humble beginnings, for in 1908 three now-forgotten men attempted test holes five to ten miles west of Tulsa, near Cushing. These were only mildly productive and sporadically operating by the time young Tom Slick arrived on the scene. Slick was twenty-nine and an agent for Charles B. Shaffer, of Chicago, charged to investigate the Tulsa area and to acquire promising leases. Shaffer and Slick were aware that predecessors had failed to find oil around Drumright, Okla-

Glenn Pool Oil Field, fifteen miles south of Tulsa, 1910. (*Courtesy of the Beryl Ford Collection, Tulsa, Oklahoma*)

homa, southeast of Tulsa, where they had drilled several dry holes at a high cost; yet they were convinced that the V-shaped valleys with narrow flood plains and outcroppings of sandstone and limestone, features of an anticline, signified the presence of petroleum-producing sand.

After numerous disappointing ventures, Slick obtained a lease from Frank Wheeler, a stone man and farmer, for a small tract of land one mile north of Drumright. Shrouding the activity in secrecy, Slick moved his rig onto the Wheeler land in January of 1911 and began drilling. Workers came to and from the site and whispered not a word about what they were doing, but such unusual happenings created mild excitement and speculation in Tulsa. Some people deduced that Slick had struck a gusher, while others laughed that he was dodging his backers by creating a mystery. Nevertheless, at the depot in mid-March he met Shaffer and an assistant, who had arrived from Chicago. After a hurried greeting they walked to a Tulsa House room, and within an hour Slick and Shaffer had discreetly rented as many horses and wagons as they could find.

Soon the word was out that on the cold, windy morning of March 10, 1912 oil had bubbled forth on Slick's claim, at first in a slow trickle and then with a burst of energy.

At first the news electrified the town, and hundreds of men tramped to the Wheeler sands, but eventually everyone discovered that the source was quite limited. Unshaken, Slick continued buying leases, and late in 1912 he alone founded the Slick Oil Company, using an initial investment of $500,000 collected from a new set of partners: B. B. Jones, a banker in Bristow, Oklahoma, and Charles J. Wrightsman, a lawyer in Tulsa. By March of 1913 the organization held more than 2,000 acres, and the first Wheeler well was producing a much larger supply of oil. The wildcatter succeeded where others had failed, primarily because he forged holes 2,347 feet deeper than previously dug.

When the *Tulsa Democrat,* a new local newspaper, reported that Wheeler Number One was producing 400, other drilling began, and within a year pump jacks worked furiously in locations surrounding the initial discovery. Early exploration took place along a line extending six miles north of Drumright, where independent oil men Tommy Atkins and Late Kalvin hit numerous strikes. Working in teams ten to twelve hours a day, prospectors filled tank after tank destined for refineries in Kansas and Texas; yet, as the land became overcrowded, owners of small firms gambled that more lay in other directions, especially after geologist Frank Buttram completed his survey of the Cushing field for the State of Oklahoma, in 1913. His findings ushered in a new era in the Cushing sands for it was concluded that the tremendous supply was inestimable; consequently the year 1913 saw increased activity. In January the field averaged 11,000, and within thirty days businesses extracted more than 20,000. B. B. Jones was the largest single producer, supplying 2,934 and earning for Jones the pleasing sum of $2.30 a minute. The McMann Oil Company stretched the perimeter of the field southward, with discoveries near present-day Oilton, Oklahoma; although the wells were not major producers, they did stimulate exploration in southwestern Oklahoma. Here drilling costs were high, for it was necessary to dig deeper, but the wells were very productive and brought in an average of 8,000. The Oklahoma Producers and Mid-River oil companies extracted tons of crude around the Cimarron riverbed, the scene of greatest activity. Bartlesville, Oklahoma, one of the later fields to open, had 160 separate locations, which generated 160,000. The Healdton sands peaked in May of 1915 with 95,000, although this resulted in lower-quality fuel than other Oklahoma crude. By October of 1916 output from the Cushing field reached 165,000 After each significant find the price dragged drastically, because the market could not absorb such huge quantities. Thus, although the new industry brought people and money into Tulsa, it also created periods of "boom and bust" in the city's economy. From a price in 1906 of fifty-nine cents for top grade, the figure plunged in 1907 to thirty-nine cents, and some petroleum sold that year for as little as twenty-three cents. Although the value soon soared, the next decade recorded another drastic drop, from $1.05 in April of 1914 to $.55 in February of 1915, and a number of operators sold below that floor. Many individuals proposed remedies, all centering on a belief that the federal government must eventually intervene.

Soon after the twin territories had joined to become Oklahoma, in 1907, state courts ruled that oil people must drill wells within thirty days after they signed a lease. The action marked an attempt to prevent unethical tycoons from limiting the supply within any given period of time, a practice that amounted to monopolistic price-fixing. The industry petitioned the federal government for aid, however, suggesting that legal restrictions hindered business development, even though many producers realized that overproduction was a major cause of their woes. To control or even create profits, therefore, those speculators who could afford the action finally decided to hold their inventories until demand made them more valuable. Finally the advent of World War I stimulated price increases, which reduced reliance on artificial attempts to manipulate values. French Prime Minister George Clemenceau confessed that oil was as important to an industrialized economy "as blood" was to human life, for to win an armed conflict a country had to have ships, trucks, and modern weapons, which required lubricants and gasoline.

As the world's major petroleum producer, the United States contributed to almost 80 percent of the Allied oil supplies. These wartime demands increased corporate profits to a national high of $1.40 by 1916, and eventually, by 1920, to $3.50. Driving to grease the war machine, conglomerates expanded operations in the Cushing field, the Glenn Pool, and throughout the world, inflating the value of virgin territory. In 1918 the Mid-Continent Petroleum Company sold eighty acres to the Katie Fisico Company for $2 million. The first five postwar years saw the value of oil and property decline, but Glenn Pool and the Cushing field remained for another decade's exploration and production beginning in 1929.

General prosperity enticed many individuals seeking personal aggrandizement to swarm into Tulsa. The success stories of a few whetted the appetites of thousands of prospective migrants by perpetuating the frontier promise of wealth and success. Such an image seduced a horde of rugged individualists who all dreamed of being oil barons. As in the cases of the California, Montana, and Colorado gold rushes during the nineteenth century, however, major corporations wrenched out the lion's share of bounty. There were exceptions. One such tale was that of Ralph A. Josey, a native Texan, who in May of 1905 sought a Tulsa "grub stake." Living on less than seven dollars a week, he struck a friendship with Jack McConnell, a wildcatter from Kansas. The two men combined their money and purchased a lease of five acres just south of the Tide Water Oil Company. Twenty-four months later they had earned almost $1 million and sold a portion of their holdings for $115,000. Similarly William H. Malliken possessed the largest section of land at Glenn Pool, a claim that yielded him 3 million total barrels.

The life of Zeke Moore, a black man, superbly reinforced the notion that in Tulsa lay anyone's chance for economic advancement. Moore was serving a sentence for horse stealing when investigators made the Glenn Pool find just west of his 125-acre farm. From prison, Moore entrusted two adventurers with the lease to his land at the height of its value, and four years later Moore walked from jail directly to his bank and collected royalties totalling $400,000.

Actually most of the seekers' tales were tragic, for people hastily organized and inadequately financed small concerns that eventually were unable to compete with enterprises having large capital support; the underfunded proved unable to sustain their operations amid a volatile market. Of those who did find wealth, a sizable number lost their fortunes in later speculative ventures and ill-conceived undertakings.

Agrarian Tulsa was quickly dying, evolving into an industrial city at a logarithmic rate. The growth was not just a matter of chance, however. Any one of a number of towns in what became southeastern Oklahoma could have experienced the pecuniary booms that reverberated in Tulsa. Civic leaders reasoned that the prospective center and subsequent controller of the oil industry would not necessarily be the city closest to the fields but the one in which the refining occurred and in which the business magnates made their homes. Tulsa futurists, therefore, schemed to construct an economic mecca and a center of political power in the southeast.

In January of 1904 M. L. Baird, J. D. Hagler, and George T. Williamson took the first step by completing a toll bridge across the Arkansas River; constructed with federal money, the steel spans and plank flooring were strong enough for any size wagon carrying tons of cargo. Transporters no longer feared the treacherous river, for the bridge closed the watery gap between oil fields west of town and the burgeoning community. Williamson, proud of the accomplishment, hung a sign that Tulsans readily understood: "You Said We Couldn't Do It, But We Did."

Next, a special Tulsa committee underwrote the construction of "Uncle Sam," the first refinery, with $5,000 and twenty free acres of land. However, unsound financing, poor transport systems, and missed opportunities ended the venture only months after its inception. The Commercial Club, the chamber of commerce forerunner, doggedly continued to influence business growth through bonus money and property contribution. In 1905 the Tulsans gave the La Tomette Smelter Company $1,735 to settle, and finally in 1913 the Commercial Club donated $2 million and 320 acres to the Waters-Pierce Oil Company, which built the first complete refinery. In 1914 the chamber of commerce invited Prairie Oil and Gas Company, a subsidiary of Standard Oil, to relocate its main offices and build a major processing plant on the outskirts of town. It later received the contract to supply natural gas to the community and remained for many years one of the largest enterprises in the state.

Payments were an accepted practice in those days, and few cities could match the effort that local Tulsa boosters made, and, as they had hoped, the enthusiasm paid off. In 1903 Tulsa consisted of 5,000 inhabitants; in 1907, 7,000; in 1910, 18,000; and by 1920,

Bird's-eye view of Tulsa, looking north from atop Tulsa High School, 1905. (*Courtesy of the Beryl Ford Collection, Tulsa, Oklahoma*)

72,000 people called the area "home." More than 100 oil and gas companies employed 15,000 field workers and averaged $15,000 in royalty payments a month. In the northern and eastern sections of the state, twenty refineries, each constructed at a cost of $2 million, operated around the clock; Gulf Coast and Atlantic Seaboard corporation pipeline investments totaled $50 million. In the single year 1911, nationally- and locally-based firms drilled 4,986 wells at a combined cost of $11,000 and lost about $800,000 on speculative sands that produced nothing but 675 dry holes. Ninety-five of the state petroleum concerns had home offices in Tulsa. Joshawa S. Cosden controlled one such firm, located on eighty acres in west Tulsa. A native of Baltimore, Maryland, he had been operating a small plant in the Osage Nation until 1911, at which time he decided to sell out and move closer to the action. In 1925 he named his refinery the Mid-Continent Petroleum Corporation, at that time one of the world's largest independents. The Williams Company was another national organization originating in Tulsa. Today it averages billions of dollars in yearly sales and assets. It began in 1915, when two brothers, David R. and S. Miller Williams, organized a manufacturing and pipeline firm.

By the end of World War I everything was new. Oil men had replaced ranchers as Tulsa moguls, just as the latter had overpowered the Creeks before them. The streets were littered with pipe and wood as construction moved at a rapid pace. Private homes fell before the symbols of progress, commercial buildings, but they were resurrected on the fields and grasslands north and east of downtown. Clinton's dream had become a reality: oil had propelled the cattle railhead into national prominence. By 1920 the unchallenged "Oil Capital of the World" supplied the lifeblood for industrial, twentieth-century America.

IV

How to Build a City

For three years after the Glenn Pool strike, the neighboring, soon-to-be Oklahoma towns of Muskogee, Bartlesville, and Stroud battled with Tulsa for the honor of being the center of oil activity. The vision of their home as a commercial oasis, added to a blustering frontier spirit, drove Tulsans to a flurry of "boostering" activities far exceeding anything their rivals could produce. The rate of population growth between 1900 and 1920 was several times that documented throughout the entire trans-Mississippi West during the same period. Precocious leaders knew that without an organizing force chaos would reign; therefore some townspeople, similar to Americans in other cities throughout the Progressive Era, became advocates of corporate reform, culture, and public service. The generally Republican-slanted *Tulsa World* and William Stryker's new Democratic-oriented *Tulsa Daily Democrat* religiously reported and took sides in most controversies, although on some occasions both shared a muckraking passion.

Although it would be easy to assume that the emergent progressive influence was liberal, numerous historians such as Richard Hofstadter have noted that the reformers' motives were rooted in politically and economically conservative tenets, and such was the case in Tulsa. Although city Democrats and Republicans battled over issues, almost every leader's goal was to preserve individual opportunities for success and fulfillment. Progressives hoped to retain, yet civilize and modernize, the frontier image, which beckoned those who longed to be masters of their own futures. Tulsa was for many the new vista, a place in which a person could apply his or her talents and training with relative assurance of ascending from a low or middle social echelon.

Oil discovery notoriety introduced thousands of Tulsans to Indians and cattle people. Although some former Confederate states such as Texas contributed to the influx of settlers, most of the community leaders who emerged from this next wave of frontiersmen hailed from the Midwest and had social roots solidly entrenched in middle-class values. They were endowed with the philosophy of thrift and hard work inherited from New England founders. Harry Campbell, who wrote most of the petition for Tulsa's incorporation, was born in Hamilton, Illinois. James M. Gillette, real estate agent and stockholder and director in the Tulsa National Bank, came from Missouri. More than one-half of the civic spokespeople in the early days came from Illinois, Ohio, and Pennsylvania.

Many of the newcomers and a few of the longtime residents took extra-governmental responsibility for the town's phenomenal growth in the early twentieth century. In March of 1901 a small cadre of enthusiasts founded the Tulsa Commercial Club, which after a decade became the chamber of commerce. Although, as mentioned in "Chapter II," one of the functions of the group was to attract oil refineries, its broader purpose was to organize the direct movements drawing manufacturing interests into the city. Under the directorship of men like George W. Mowbray, the first president, and James Hall, "the father of modern Tulsa," the organization influenced landowners to donate rights-of-way for incoming railroads and to supply thousands of dollars as bonuses to corporations. Truly the chamber was even more influential in Tulsa than was the city government, for it changed the town's personality until it resembled a community that they had somehow uprooted and transported from Ohio or Illinois to Indian Territory.

The popularly dubbed "boosters" had their problems in the beginning, for in 1905 oil wells around Bartlesville, north of Tulsa, produced copious crude supplies; and Muskogee, to the southeast, claimed a population larger than that of Tulsa. To the southwest, Cushing's citizens proved to be so accommodating to oil men operating in the town's field that even the *Tulsa Daily World* grudgingly admitted that the little hamlet bordered on becoming the "queen of the oil fields." Most Indian Territory residents believed that Tulsans suffered from delusions of grandeur, and critics delighted in deriding promoters' attempts to attract attention.

Ridicule only made Tulsans stronger and more determined to overcome the initial advantage of other towns. The collective Commercial Club mind spawned a myriad of schemes. The coterie paid $5,000 to the *St. Louis Star* for a feature page illustrating Tulsa's modern advancements. Any visiting dignitary received red-carpet treatment, which usually consisted of beef barbecued over an open gas well, a chautauqua-style lecture, and a medley of patriotic songs, which the club band performed. While such activities served to impress visitors, local publishing firms contracted for various booklets designed to educate locals about the wide range of attractions that their town offered. Done on expensive paper and securely bound, the contents varied from vapid statistics on agricultural output to bombastic praise. The Commercial Club-authored pamphlets, such as *Facts About Tulsa: A Coming Metropolis,* appeared in local newspapers or sold for a nominal price. Although the first known history of Tulsa, printed in 1903, included numerous objective facts, it nonetheless presented a glowing account of the town. The written word was therefore a crucial early promotional technique. In 1915 the chamber of commerce carried on the tradition by publishing a magazine entitled *Tulsa Spirit,* which featured stories about economic growth and cultural enrichment.

Such efforts rewarded Tulsans with considerable success as long as their schemes stayed within a realistic realm. Some plots were a bit ridiculous, however, exposing the club members' glee over their own audacity. In 1907 they boldly invited national Democratic Party leaders to hold the national convention in Tulsa. On behalf of the townspeople they promised a bonus of $100,000 and a new auditorium specially constructed for the party of Andrew Jackson and William Jennings Bryan. Unfortunately the Democratic Central Committee decided that Baltimore, Maryland, was better equipped to accommodate delegates from across the nation. Unashamed, the town's leadership saw the negative response as more a Democratic Party than a Tulsa loss and intensified its efforts by urging locals to "write friends; tell them of wonderful Tulsa." Never at a loss for a novel gimmick, the Commercial Club advanced its cause by authorizing the Paragon Feature Film Company to make a three-reel movie about Tulsa and the surrounding oil fields. The final agreement stipulated that the producers would receive $1,000 and that the Commercial Club would reap any revenue above that fee. Subsequently, the *Oklahoma City Times* praised the community for "making the greatest advertising efforts in the history of the state."

Undoubtedly three booster railroad excursions, in 1903, 1905, and 1907, were the most ingenious maneuvers that brought Tulsa national publicity. The first Commercial Club train traveled to St. Louis in connection with the Indian Territory Day celebration. The party consisted of seventy-five men and a hurriedly organized "Indian," Ray-Funk-directed, fifteen-piece band. Funk was a barber, but his group (which did not have in it a single Indian) performed brilliantly and proved to be a major attraction. When onlookers asked why the entertainers' skins were so pale, Funk retorted that the musicians were "civilized Indians and came along to demonstrate how Americanized the territory had become." Such harmless deceit won considerable notoriety for Tulsa. One moment of unexpected embarrassment, however, came when Clyde Lynch, the tour organizer, asked Arkansas representatives to lend the orchestra a few apples, peaches, plums, and grapes for a local fruit display contest. The wayfarers won a blue ribbon, and when the Tulsa papers, ignorant of what had transpired, heralded their town as "the prize fruit-growing center of the promising Indian Territory," Arkansans fumed.

The second journey, in 1905, ranked as an unmatched achievement. Composed of 100 of the town's leading citizens, the train embarked on March 13 for Pacific, Missouri, the first stop along a 2,000-mile route throughout the Midwest and Northwest. Describing it as a benefit "for every property owner in town," wives and children worked throughout the night the day before departure, decorating it with banners and streamers. The train carried representatives from the Commercial Club, exhibits of what one could purchase in town, a printing press, and an employee of the *Tulsa Daily Democrat,* who printed leaflets describing the wonders of Tulsa. The sojourners distributed them to the welcoming crowds at every stop. More interested in attracting attention than in talking business with civic leaders of other communities, the boosters tried to create a carnival atmosphere wherever they stopped. The orchestra presented lively patriotic marches, while a gangling young cowboy named Will Rogers amazed audiences with his fancy rope tricks.

The trip was not without hazard. One evening while Tulsans banqueted in Terre Haute, Indiana, owners of a local brewery, taken with the Southwesterners, filled the baggage coach with enough beer to provide every booster with three each day during the remainder of the tour. Some thirsty excursionists, however, preferred to drink it all as quickly as possible, causing much dissension among the group, not to mention intoxication. Clyde Lynch, organizer of the trip, formed a committee of trusted friends consisting of himself, Emmett Smiley, Mel Baird, and R. T. Epperson; stealing into the baggage car while the other passengers slept in alcoholic stupor, they threw the contents, case by case, onto the Indiana countryside. There is no record of what transpired on board the train the next morning when the passengers discovered the loss of their liquor, but all members returned home safe.

In Chicago the Tulsans had a more serious encounter. The sides of the Pullman cars bore banners proudly proclaiming the purpose of the trip, but depot officials of the windy city took a dim view of the clutter, and Chicago authorities ordered the signs removed. The Tulsans defiantly refused, contending that they had paid for the railroad's services in addition to the right to decorate within reason. Fearing that the situation might lead to open hostilities, a unit of the Chicago police arrived on the scene to mediate the dispute. In response, the Indian Territory band climbed to the top of the train and proceeded to play a concert, much to the enjoyment of the crowd. The large audience gathering along the tracks blocked train service. Finally out of desperation the railroad personnel compromised, stating that if the travelers would remove the signs until the train left Chicago they could then put them back on. One city employee disgustedly remarked, "When they leave, I don't care if they run this train to hell and back, if [they] want to." When the engineer finally pulled slowly out of the station, the crowd cheered. Obviously the incident had not darkened the favorable impression Tulsans had made on Chicagoans.

Many large metropolitan newspapers poked fun at the Indian Territory promoters, but Tulsans took it in stride. After all, they wanted recognition, and they got it. Several newspapers, however, reacted more soberly. "Down in Tulsa," said the *St. Louis Post-Dispatch* editor, "they have a theory that whatever helps the town helps the citizens. It's a pretty good theory, too. It makes nations as well as cities great." In a March 22 *Chicago Inter-Ocean* editorial, commentators wrote, "Keep your eye on Tulsa; we will."

The final envoy was the most elaborately organized and was the longest of the three. The sixteen-day venture covered more than 2,500 miles: from Tulsa to St. Louis, north to Chicago, east to New York City, and then to the nation's capital, reaching fifteen states and the District of Columbia. The specially commissioned railcar carried cargo similar to that previously taken. At every stop, local dignitaries greeted the ensemble and entertained it lavishly from the time the train pulled into a station until it departed. Representatives of commercial clubs, city officials, uniformed receptionists, and state dignitaries came from all areas of the nation to partake of the fun. In Washington, D.C., President Theodore

One hundred Tulsa boosters, 1905, visiting eastern cities and promoting Tulsa, Indian Territory. Will Rogers was their group entertainer (in white shirtsleeves at far right). (*Courtesy of the Beryl Ford Collection, Tulsa, Oklahoma*)

Roosevelt tendered a party for the boosters, and a joint session of Congress gave them a standing ovation in appreciation of their ingenuity and progressiveness. The governor of New York welcomed Tulsans at Union Station. State and local officials paraded them down Fifth Avenue, past thousands of cheering New Yorkers. Not to be outdone, Chicagoans stopped the wires of the Chicago Board of Trade for the only time in history while the Commercial Club band performed the most popular songs of the day.

The extravaganzas worked because they attracted notable people to Tulsa. Robert T. Daniel, a multimillionaire land developer from Miami, Florida, came to build the ten-story Daniel building and the modern Tulsa Hotel, after reading news accounts of the 1905 expedition. The enthusiasm so impressed mine operator George Bayne from Joplin, Missouri, that he decided to see what they were bragging about. Within a matter of days after arriving, he began investing in utilities and in September of 1905 helped Eugene Lorton purchase the *Tulsa World* and renamed it the *Tulsa Daily World*.

The community leadership understood, however, that if Tulsa were to remain the center of the feverish activity in the Mid-Continent field the first business target had to be the railroads, for only with a modern transportation system could they hope to accommodate the demands of national free enterprise. Unfortunately the Frisco was Tulsa's lone railway, so the Commercial Club began seeking another.

The aroused sense of urgency coincided with plans of the owners of the Missouri, Kansas, and Texas Railroad Company. In 1902 surveyors for the MK&T (Katy), intending to connect with the main line running from Parsons, Kansas, to Oklahoma City, began working at Wybark, a small community north of Muskogee. The secondary line intersected the Frisco track seven miles east of Tulsa. Katy engineers alerted Tulsa's leaders, who knew that if the railroad bypassed the town it meant death for the struggling community. The Commercial Club held an emergency meeting and chose a committee consisting of S. G. Kennedy, W. F. Jones, M. J. Romine, and T. E. Smiley to meet with company representatives and try to persuade them to run their line through Tulsa. Following the usual practice, the Tulsans brought the railroad employees to town within a matter of days and held an honorary banquet. Such "friendly persuasion" impressed the guests, and they pledged to survey a feasible line intersecting the town. Unfortunately the workers acted against the wishes of their superiors, who fired the surveyors for insubordination.

The Commercial Club refused to let the expulsion be the final word. Kennedy, George W. Mowbray, Sr., and Joe Price, of St. Louis, visited the president of the MK&T. The three emissaries faced the railroad heads, who rested behind a huge mahogany desk, and presented their most powerful argument. Over the past twenty years, they pointed out, the Frisco had done more business than the company could readily handle, and once oil began flowing from Red Fork the railroad business would be a bonanza. Tulsa already was feeling the first influx of people, the spokesmen continued, and these were not only oil prospectors but also potential store owners and property agents, bankers, and consumers of goods that the Katy could haul. Next, the company's chief engineer, from Yale, Indian Territory, testified that according to the unauthorized survey, the grade A line to Tulsa could be constructed more cheaply than the one originally considered. If the Katy officials would reconsider, Mowbray interrupted, he and four Tulsa businessmen would serve as trustees for a $12,000 bonus and furnish the right-of-way, a proposition worth $15,000. All railroad companies and major businesses expected gratuities as part of any deal, but this one was more generous than the Katy owners had reason to expect from such a small community. After short deliberation the two parties signed an agreement stating that engineer W. H. Hendren would lay the Wybark-to-Osage extension through Tulsa.

Residents were elated at this success, but the year 1903 saw increased tensions and competition with nearby towns when the two Red Fork strikes startled the territory. Closer to Red Fork than its rivals, Tulsa heard the news first, and city leaders immediately knew that two railroad lines were not enough to corner the oil business. The Commercial Club also heard that Charles N. Haskell, the future governor of Oklahoma and principal promoter of the Midland Valley Railroad Company, intended to construct a track from Muskogee to Arkansas City, Kansas, by way of Sapulpa, Indian Territory, and Red Fork. He would thereby establish the Midland Valley as the major carrier of petroleum. Fearful that their time and energies might go unrewarded if Sapulpa should lie on the new path, a group of businessmen went to Muskogee to interview Haskell. After lengthy negotiations he agreed that a Tulsa route was the cheapest one; and if that was not enough incentive, the citizens once more dug deep into their pockets and granted Haskell a $15,000 reward for changing his mind.

Competition among the three transportation companies later became so fierce that within two years Tulsa warehouses received rebates from Midland Valley that over the years more than compensated for the initial bonus. Thus by 1903 Tulsa had three transport systems from which it was able to stake its claim as the center of the oil industry. The intense rivalry and good market finally attracted the Santa Fe Railroad Company, which Tulsans had tried for years to coax. At the height of the rush for oil on Ida Glenn's farm, James Dunn, chief organizer for the Santa Fe, appeared in Tulsa. Known as a shrewd man, he had extracted an agreement from Midland Valley that if Dunn should decide to recommend a line to his superiors, the Santa Fe could use its tracks and depot. The hustle and bustle in the streets convinced him that it would be to the company's advantage to build its own facilities. Within twenty-four hours he told the Commercial Club that Santa Fe would budge for a $12,000 fee, and the Tulsans quickly accepted the offer. The advantages of having a fourth major railroad were obvious. Visions of freight yards with oil tankers lined end-to-end as far as the eye could see, not to mention the hundreds of people coming and going daily, taking mental pictures of Tulsa with them wherever they went, ran through the heads of the civic leaders. With the Santa Fe making regular stops, Tulsa could dominate the petroleum industry. The vision became reality in September 1905 when the company opened its latest extension, and the presence of extensive first-rate transportation tied Tulsa to the oil fields, making it the major distributing point for petroleum throughout the Southwest.

Robert H. Hall, son of Harry C. Hall, forged additional national ties by establishing the first telephone exchange in 1903. Although Hall began with fewer than 100 subscribers, the invention was so revolutionary that it was only a matter of time before thousands of people would have one of the new gadgets. In 1904 the daily newspapers frequently ran columns explaining how to use them. Hall operated the office until 1906, when he sold his enterprise to the Indian Territory Telephone Company, of what shortly became Vinita, Oklahoma. Tulsa contracted with the firm for a period of twenty years and published the first directory in 1906. Early telephone business rates were by today's standards astonishingly low. Under the agreement, monthly charges could not exceed $1.50 for residential phones and $2.50 for business hookups. Southwestern Bell, a subsidiary of Bell Telephone and Telegraph System, arrived in Tulsa and bought Indian Territory Company holdings in 1912. That year the city had 2,000 stations; in 1921, that number had grown to 18,000, an increase of such magnitude that the company created the Tulsa district in October of 1920, and John N. Wobler was the first general manager.

As railroads and telephones linked Tulsa to the nation, the city's financial community exibited growing strength. In 1903 the community had four banks with a total capital stock of just over $250,000. William H. Halsell and Jay Forsythe owned the First National Bank, which controlled the largest holdings–$117,835. In 1905 two new ones opened–the Farmer's National Bank, recording deposits of $85,394, and the Bank of Commerce, boasting $130,000 in capital; in that year, also, the First National moved to Second and Main into the five-story "skyscraper of Mid-Continent" featuring Tulsa's first elevator. The first lending firms were accustomed to the stable, no-nonsense fiscal policies associated with ranching and therefore perceived the "fly-by-night" oil men, with their dreams of hidden wealth, as lunatics. To combat the fiscal conservatism, petroleum investors opened their own local banks and brought high financing to Tulsa. When Harry F. Sinclair and Pat J. White reopened the old Farmer's National as the new Exchange National Bank with an initial capital of $400,000.00, the first day of business saw $424,674.14 in deposits. Other institutions soon fell into line or faced ruin. To minimize risk, however, and still service the customer, Sinclair and White appointed oil people to the board of directors. Soon the petroleum industry was receiving ample support from local banks, and by the beginning of the 1920s Tulsa money houses had overcome the initial advantage of Eastern establishments.

While local bankers adapted to the new environment, the construction and real estate agencies joined in a cooperative effort to build new living accommodations. Within a few months after the

Glenn Pool strike, William N. Robinson opened his still-unfinished hotel at the corner of Third and Main. During the early days of the oil boom the Robinson Hotel served as a temporary home for tycoons from across the United States. It was the place with clean sheets, good food, and speedy service. No doubt hundreds of monetary matters were settled within its walls; in fact, the story persists that the White-Sinclair Oil Company, at one time the largest independent petroleum firm in the world, originated shortly after Sinclair had walked pajama-clad down the hall from his room to the lavatory. The hotel, the finest west of the Mississippi and east of the Rocky Mountains, had five stories, with 126 rooms and an elevator.

Activity in real estate increased in proportion to the growing demand. In 1904 there were four agencies in Tulsa searching for land that was hard to find. Within a year after Glenn Pool, Tulsa suffered its first housing problem. City limits made it too small for its exploding population, and the competition for homes was fierce. The Northern Realty and Abstract Company urged prospective landowners, "Don't trust your own judgment," lest they fall prey to charlatans and thieves. The Oil and Gas Real Estate Company, as did its competitors, cried for local officials to extend Tulsa boundaries, saying, "We have more clients than property."

The city did gradually annex more land, and by the decade's end Tulsa had miraculously metamorphized. If one walked south of the Frisco tracks along Main Street, he or she passed the Oil Well Supply Company, a store catering strictly to the new industry. The three-story Baxter Furniture Company, one of the first in town, stood on the corner of First and Main, with the New State Hotel at Second and Main. Next door to Baxter's the Wright Clothing Company featured the "best in dress" but had stiff competition from Lynch and Calhoun Men's Store, in which one could purchase the "finest of hats." If a person needed equipment ranging from household utensils to used oil-field pipes, Hale and Reynolds Hardware was the place to go, although Hall General Store had also earned a solid reputation over the years. What neither of these places had, Trees Brothers probably did; moreover, the National Supply sold everything from wrenches to overalls. City Bank, another financial establishment, marked the end of First Street, and the Robinson Hotel did the same for the southern end of Main.

Neither was far from the community's leading firm, the First National Bank.

Downtown shoppers purchased salt-cured roast and newly plucked chicken, not to mention fresh vegetables when they were in season, at Morrison and Son's Grocery, a sign that the community was no longer self-sustaining. The town served as the breadbasket for oil men who, unlike the Creeks, ranchers, and farmers, could not grow their own food. Thus the course of local agriculture had changed as merchants and husbandrymen supplied foodstuff, at skyrocketing prices. Beef and vegetables, formerly sold to only Kansas City or St. Louis, now had a market in Tulsa, and the demand for food increased constantly.

Sells Drug and Reeder's Pharmacy now sold patent medicines to cure all varieties of afflictions. Enamored with progress, oldtimers laughed recalling the days that the substance now being fanatically pumped from the ground had been used both internally and externally as the "miracle drug of the century;" yet many of the "modern" ointments, pills, and lotions sold over the counter were just as fraudulent as had been the petroleum medicines of bygone days.

In 1910 John and Cass Allen Mayo, furniture store owners from Missouri, built a five-story edifice at Fifth and Main. Within seven years ground-floor expansion and an additional five stories completed the Mayo building. The pair kept the furniture store on the first floor and rented the remaining nine stories for office space. Residents considered it a monument to Tulsa, transformed. Shortly before World War I thirty-two passenger and freight trains arrived and departed daily, bringing new people and products from all sections of the United States. Tourists had a choice of twenty hotels; each of two of them, the old Robinson and the new Hotel Tulsa, was six stories high. In 1917 and 1918 the increasing demand for office space resulted in two "skyscrapers," the ten-story Kennedy and the sixteen-story Cosden office buildings.

Many Tulsans shared the conviction that public services must accompany economic growth in any "civilized" American city. Even before the public auction that followed the town's incorporation in 1901, initiators had busily gone to the rescue of the Presbyterian Mission School. Early in 1899 the Presbyterian Board had sold its property and holdings to the Creek Nation, thus creating the first public school. Funds for the transaction came from the formerly noted Tulsa Banking Company, soon to be the First National Bank, but Jay Forsythe, R. N. Cynum, Joe Price, and James Hall personally guaranteed the loan. In May an election produced the first school board, consisting of Hall, J. D. Hagler, B. F. Colley, J. M. Morrow, P. L. Price, and T. E. Smiley. These citizens, like many of the other trailblazers who joined them during the new century's first two decades, believed that education led to spiraling social advancement. A number of the Commercial Club members had at least some college education; many were physicians and attorneys; and numerous business magnates were highly learned. For instance, First National Bank director Leonard M. Poe was a law school graduate, and before taking the executive's position he had been a judge.

The year 1902 was one filled with purpose for the civic-oriented founders. A popularly elected council called the City Commission wrote a charter forming a local government and empowered itself to enact ordinances. It levied taxes on real estate for municipal undertakings. One of the first projects was to purchase the Creek-Nation-owned school, for $426.43, and almost immediately the school board contracted carpenters for $1.50 a day to add rooms and a second story to the original structure.

In 1906 a new combined eleven-room grade and twenty-one-room high school opened, but only after a heated polemic involving north- and south-side inhabitants who wanted the institution located in their areas. The board resolved to work for bond issues of $25,000 to build the north's primary school and $50,000 to construct the upper-grades facility to be located south, on the old Presbyterian Mission site. The high school had an auditorium and a dome, features that developers used to sell the town as a modern city. The first senior class graduated one boy and three girls, in 1906, but the total enrollment was 1,100 and climbed quickly in one year to 1,792. Crowded conditions therefore forced another referendum, which sanctioned $25,000 for two additional grade schools.

In response to the Oklahoma State Constitution, which twin territorial representatives framed in 1908, every city with more than 2,000 people had to form a new charter. Authors placed the Tulsa school system under a district board of education, which replaced the city government's role. Positive about the future, that same year faculty and citizens organized the Parent-Teacher Association, and Charles W. Grimes became the first county superintendent. He, too, was hopeful and drew district boundaries much larger than the existing city size, to take in rapidly expanding subdivisions.

A major controversy erupted in the summer of 1908, when media sources reported that Tulsa education buildings were in critical condition and that they still belonged to the city, not the district. Citizens feared that the structures might become public halls, fire stations, or jails; and schools were already bursting at the seams with children. Tulsans resolved the problem by passing, in 1909, a $230,000 bond proposal; $105,000 paid the city for existing facilities, and the rest funded Washington, Lincoln, and Irving schools. Townspeople continued to act with celerity; during the next ten years they bequeathed $750,000 to remodel the aforementioned three schools and build Clinton, Horace Mann, Kendall, Osage, Riverview, and Sequoyah schools. In addition, the first educational bond measure for $1 million passed in May of 1919.

After statehood Tulsa legally segregated both black students and black teachers from all others working or participating in the school system. The town financed facilities and salaries with special levies primarily extracted from black citizens. In 1909 the school board built Dunbar grade school, and others such as Bunche, Johnson, and South Haven followed. The board soon founded Carver Junior High; and finally in 1913 Booker T. Washington Senior High provided the first available secondary education for fourteen black students.

Another innovation was the Clinton primary facility, which reflected board member H. O. McClure's "unit system." He utilized real estate effectively by purchasing a block of land for the structure and designing it with a courtyard in the center. A booster trip to Chicago had influenced McClure to migrate, and he contributed much to volunteer community endeavors and also established the McClure Hardware Company.

The preoccupation with education led to the notion that Tulsa needed a first-rate institution of higher learning. Young adults could then obtain college training without leaving town, thereby keeping intelligence and money within the city limits. The school would also attract exceptional individuals from throughout the nation. Locals postulated that perhaps after sampling all that Tulsa had to offer, out-of-state students might decide to take up residence after graduation.

During the first decade of the twentieth century the Commercial Club immediately took the lead in searching for higher educators. After months of conscientious investigation, the Club's prime target became Henry Kendall College, located in Muskogee. James Hall became chairman of a temporary committee empowered to make the college board of trustees a substantial offer. Tulsans had raised $100,000 by selling chances on residential lots at $300 each and used the money to buy tracts of prairie land on the east side of town. In addition to a campus site, Hall promised the educators an endowment of $250,000 and thirty acres, which the administration could use as it deemed necessary. Kendall officials were unable to refuse such inducements and signed an agreement

Kendall Hall, first building on present-day University of Tulsa campus; completed in 1908, and razed in 1972. (*Courtesy of the Beryl Ford Collection, Tulsa, Oklahoma*)

in 1907. Within a few years regents changed the name to Tulsa University, and citizens displayed their loyalty by pledging $200,000 for a permanent endowment. By 1920, although the institution was privately supported, it rivaled as a seat of higher learning the state's land-grant college in Stillwater and the University of Oklahoma in Norman.

Although stimulating the educational drive was one of the Commercial Club's and the city council's first ventures, organizers were equally concerned with other service areas. In 1901 the City Commission appointed a town marshal and granted him the power to collect misdemeanor fines. A board of health, established in April of 1901, regulated sanitary conditions, sewer systems, and construction; and assessed penalties for throwing garbage in the street or raising hogs in town. Local officials even hired a trained city superintendent of health for the sumptuous retainer of $100.

Most of Tulsa's turn-of-the-century buildings were made of lumber, making potential fires a serious problem. On the night of June 6, 1900, a group of people met to organize a fire department. They elected Richard C. Alder as chief because he was the only person present who had had previous experience, in his hometown of Springfield, Missouri. The nonprofessional fire fighters earned $.05 per hour and an extra $1.50 when they actually combatted a blaze. Within a few years the city led the new state in quality prevention, with a salaried fire chief, an alarm telegraph system, a machine-powered pumping engine, and the only completely motorized department in the territory.

The city council also contributed to Tulsa's contemporary appearance. The pre-statehood city charter decreed sidewalks had to be twelve feet wide in the business area and five feet wide in the residential end of town; the first ones, however, made of wooden planks, were potentially harmful because of splinters. Public safety took a step forward, though, when the voters passed a council-inspired ordinance in 1903 specifying that all walkways must be constructed of flat brick, asphalt, or cement. In 1902 city workers paved First and Second streets with brick. Although there were ten such avenues in 1904, *Democrat* editors reported that they were in poor condition. By 1907, however, Main Street had been transformed from a dry, dusty road in summer or an impassable mudhole in winter to an asphalt byway.

Looking south on Main Street near First Street, Tulsa, 1907. (*Courtesy of the Beryl Ford Collection, Tulsa, Oklahoma*)

New roadways soon became a hot political issue between rural and urban dwellers. Hard surfaces harmed animal hooves, thereby harassing the primary source of transportation for those who lived in the country, but they were essential for automobiles. Riders complained that cars frightened their horses, causing the steeds to buck or run away if left untied. Residents therefore sanctioned an eight-mile-per-hour speed limit for automobiles or any other machines that were powered by steam, gasoline, or electricity. Persons on horseback had the right-of-way at intersections for several years, and violators paid fines of $1,000 or spent ninety days in the city jail. By 1909 oil people pushed for a reduction of fines and a new twenty-mile-per-hour limit. Here was just one more example illustrating Tulsa's evolution from an agriculturally- to an industrially-dominated center.

As early as 1906 the local government had annexed land between M, Osage, Elgin, and Archer avenues—what today is called North Tulsa. It soon became apparent that Tulsans sorely needed some uniform code for laying out additions to the city. When the engineers resurveyed the townsite for the new charter, in 1908, the city proposed a referendum outlining the steps to be taken in adding new areas to the community. An engineer plotted the land, and the mayor and council approved of the blueprint. All streets came under the same regulations, depending on whether they were to be in a residential or a business district. To make transportation more expedient for visitors and inhabitants alike, the public also passed ordinances regulating the naming and numbering of houses and streets. Main Street, running north and south, divided Tulsa into east and west sections, while Lawton, extending perpendicular to Main, divided the town into north and south. To bring order to the house-numbering system all residences on the west side of a street received even, and those on the east side, odd, numbers. By the beginning of World War I the city had seventy-one miles of paved byways, a far cry from the old dirt avenues characteristic of the century's first few years.

Realizing that contemporizing the city would require governmental and corporate cooperation, the city council and the chamber joined forces, especially during the first decade of the century, in an attempt to mold a planned environment. By the century's second decade the latter had ceased frantically attempting to draw anyone to Tulsa, even though the population continued to expand. By 1910 promoters used discretion in choosing what type of industry best suited Tulsa's needs. Now the citizenry passed laws prohibiting mining, oil prospecting, and drilling for natural gas within city boundaries. Despite the impression that anyone was welcome, such was not the case. Officials hoped to keep as much industry as possible south of the Arkansas River, and if that was not always possible, then other semi-distant locations served.

The chamber continued to print literature praising the advantages of moving to the area and sent the material to selected prospective companies. Almost always, chamber members and public servants sent an investigating team, which inspected an interested business. If both the company and Tulsa found the situation agreeable, negotiations began immediately. Naturally, if Tulsans wanted corporations, plenty of bonus money sweetened deals, for the chamber policy recognized that when all other considerations were equal the town that won the firm would be the one with the best all-around offer. The Hurbert J. Hurrle Window Glass Company came to Tulsa because it received a five-year guarantee of three-cent natural gas for fuel and a $5,000 bonus; the Queen Bee Stove Company and the Robinson Packer and Machine Company obtained preferred locations and $5,000 each to start. By 1920 the city government could proudly state that it had granted in the year 1919 a total of $9,473,443 worth of building permits, thereby reaping at least one of the benefits of economic growth. June of that year saw the largest growth rate of any month in Tulsa history, as future companies paid more than $2,219,000 for consent forms. The federal government estimated that the city spent $1 million per month on improving downtown buildings that year.

Burgeoning Tulsa was not without its problems, two of which were an inadequate water supply and a poor sewage system. Prior

Tulsa Fire Department displaying new motorized pumper truck along with horse-drawn fire units. The fire station building, at 111 west Second Street, also housed city offices, the police department, and the jail. Tulsa, 1908. (*Courtesy of the Beryl Ford Collection, Tulsa, Oklahoma*)

Tulsa Frisco Railroad depot, 1910. (*Courtesy of the Beryl Ford Collection, Tulsa, Oklahoma*)

to the days of public service the council contracted jobs with private companies on the basis of bidding. Competition was fierce, and often, to present low estimates, organizations cut not only their overhead but also the quality of service. The Tulsa Water Company, the first to close a deal, unfortunately could not supply enough water from three wells along the Arkansas River to meet the demands. The only sewer system was one that dumped dwellers' waste into the Arkansas River, thus forcing the town to import bottled drinking and bathing water.

In 1908 the city government established a Department of City Waterworks composed of three commissioners and a superintendent, hired at $1,500 each per year. At the same time, Tulsa floated a bond issue of $125,000 to fund a new arrangement with George G. Bayne, the *World* editor. Bayne sank three holes adjacent to the river and funneled water through his privately owned pipeline, but the wells proved to be insufficient to meet ever-increasing needs. Over the next three years council-hired workers discovered five new sources on the George J. Murphy acreage; however, these were not always plentiful because they originated from

Tulsa Fire Department, 111 west Second Street, 1912. (*Courtesy of the Beryl Ford Collection, Tulsa, Oklahoma*)

the sometimes copious, and on other occasions dry, river. Supplies remained inadequate for decades and threatened Tulsa's economic stability and physical survival.

After World War I, city stewards continued to search for more bounteous underground springs; within a few months they set sights on Lake Spavinaw, fifty miles northeast of the city. Although this reservoir was smaller than most surrounding northeastern Oklahoma, inspectors determined that it could provide more than enough water for current and projected use. Mayor Charles H. Hubbard supported, and the chamber wholeheartedly endorsed, a bond election on July 10, 1919. Favorable advertising appeared in local newspapers, and the chamber initiated an "education campaign" as it had for numerous past public designs. A sizable minority objected to the plan, but the final vote was 2,340 in favor and 1,522 opposed. The city had committed itself to finance the sale of $5 million worth of securities at 5 percent annual interest to fund the construction of a series of pipelines and a water processing plant.

Tulsa taskmasters promoted, and voters approved, a new set

Bird's-eye view of Tulsa, looking north from atop Tulsa High School, 1912. Hotel Tulsa at Third & Cincinnati is the large building under construction at right. (*Courtesy of the Beryl Ford Collection, Tulsa, Oklahoma*)

of water bonds totaling $6,800,000 in November of 1921, but a stumbling block came from the Supreme Court of Oklahoma. Justices ruled that the enactment was a violation of the 1908 city charter, which stipulated that any water source must be within a five-mile, city-limit radius. Mayor Hubbard and a small cadre of Tulsans convinced Governor James B. Robertson to sanction a prospective amendment authorizing Tulsa to obtain water from any distance and empowering a special board and commissioner to manage monetary outlays for the Spavinaw program. The resolution passed in a popular city election in January of 1922, and by April of that year the expenditure of $1 million had paid for opening dam construction. Tulsa operatives erected a pumping and filtration station northeast of the city, at Mohawk Park Lakes, to fill a high-pressure lake on Reservoir Hill, and the first nectar flowed into Tulsa's veins in 1925.

Other utilities, such as natural gas and electricity, came from private companies under contract with Tulsa. Osage Natural Gas

Company supplied the former, after a March 1904 agreement. Although owners later changed the name, the original bargain arranged for two decades of service. A 1905 dispute erupted when the citizenry protested against a rate hike resulting in twenty-five cents for a thousand cubic feet. Robert Galbreath and Frank Chesley, of Glenn Pool fame, remedied the problem by establishing the People's Gas Company, which charged only twenty cents. Free enterprise thus brought competition. On December 1, 1906, Osage and Oklahoma Gas Company managers announced a fifteen-cent reduction. The markdown was too much for People's Gas, which sold out to competitors. Even so, Osage later raised its fee to sixteen. Oklahoma Natural Gas Company, however, began doing business in 1909 and once again undercut the Osage price. These two companies were the only suppliers, allotting service at a reasonable twenty and one-half cents. The city's working relationship with the Tulsa Commercial Bridge Company, which in 1904 began generating electricity, was also relatively harmonious. Bills were based on the number of watts and the amount of time used. After nine years of quality service, the corporation sold out to Public Service Company.

The Tulsa government and street railway system partnership was not pleasant. Eager to have a public transportation system, city functionaries awarded the first franchise to eighteen locals who worked diligently to uphold their end of the compact but who were unfortunately ignorant of how to fashion a railway. To rescue themselves, the Tulsans sold out for $5,000 to Charles N. Bosler, a streetcar man from Dayton, Ohio, who started the Tulsa Streetcar Company. At first the city council was reluctant, but it had spent so much time and money to get the project under way that the body eventually reached a bargain requiring Bosler to begin laying track within sixty days. The Ohioan met the requirement by laying two tracks near First Street, and an electric car made its first run along east First in May of 1907. All sides were satisfied until new settlers opened the Lynch-Forsythe addition, on Tulsa's east side. In return for service to the new section, Bosler grasped another $10,000 and a guaranteed 15 percent of all lot sales revenue. Although occupants paid the agreed amount, Bosler did not complete the venture for several years. Meanwhile other citizens complained of lax scheduling and inferior equipment. The rapidly mounting hostility between the city council and Bosler mushroomed into a heated confrontation. The commissioners charged him with reneging on an oath, and Bosler countered that the officials had made continuous, unreasonable demands for expansion. Trouble persisted until 1929, at which time Bosler sold the franchise to the United Service Company, thus ending the verbal bantering, but not Tulsa's quest for adequate mass transit.

Turn-of-the-century Tulsans also made known their need for more spiritual and intellectual communal services, namely religious and cultural. The old Presbyterian Church experienced continual success; the North Methodist held seats for 300; and the Methodist South reported that it had "a fine brick building with the largest audience room of any building in town, except for the opera hall."

Social clubs were also becoming popular. In 1903 Mrs. W. Cook and five other charter members formed the Thimble Club, which hosted receptions, teas, parties, and other festivities to honor visitors or family members. Three years later Mary E. Green founded a literary society, the Tulsa Women's Club. By the end of the decade it took up the work of Mrs. J. D. Seaman who for five years had struggled to raise money for a local library. The group managed to get the issue placed on yet another ballot, in 1910. Already laboring under a heavy tax burden, Tulsans registered their opposition at the polls. By 1913, with rivers of oil revenue coming into town, the women's Tulsa Library Association managed to raise enough money to organize a Central Public Library. The coalition prevailed on the Carnegie Foundation for a $55,000 donation, hardly suitable for the growing community, to expand and stock the building. The charity contribution helped improve the accommodations and paid a salary to Walter Ahlum, Tulsa's first trained librarian.

The social consciousness of couples such as physician Fred S. Clinton (of Red Fork fame) and Jane Heard Clinton also contributed greatly to the soul of Tulsa. One of the few leading businessmen native to the area, Clinton was born near Okmulgee, Indian Territory, on April 15, 1874. His father, a farmer-rancher, died when his son was fourteen, leaving a widow and four children. Although Clinton grew up in a rural area, as an adult his ambitions turned his career interests from being a farmer to studying medicine, making investments, and building a city. First he attended Young Harris College in Georgia. He completed his undergraduate training and married Jane Heard, the daughter of a prominent family in Elburton, Georgia. Clinton then entered the Kansas City, Missouri, College of Pharmacy and Allied Sciences, received his degree in 1896, and interned at Kansas City University Medical College one year later.

The Clintons returned to Red Fork in 1897 and formed an extremely successful partnership with physician J. C. W. Bland. Fred Clinton quickly became known throughout the land for his competency when a severe smallpox epidemic raged over the area. By 1905 he was helping to build Tulsa's first permanent medical building and nurses' training school, and in 1915 he was the prime mover in the drive to construct the ultra-modern Oklahoma Hospital. Although his life was strenuous, he still found time to represent Indian Territory in the National Red Cross and to serve a term as president of the regional Medical Association. For these and other contributions his national professional colleagues honored him in the 1926 edition of *Who's Who in American Medicine*. He actively participated in chamber activities and went on all three booster trips. Clinton was acutely interested in local history and contributed numerous articles to the Oklahoma State Historical Society journal, the *Chronicles of Oklahoma*.

One of Jane Heard Clinton's projects involved the Hyechka Club, the most famous and active of all of Tulsa's early organizations. In October of 1904 ten women founded the society in Mrs. Will Short's studio, located over John L. Sell's drugstore, at 110 South Main Street. Participants elected Clinton president and selected "Hyechka," the Creek generic word for "music," because it reflected their intentions to cultivate aesthetic appreciation in homes, schools, and churches. With the first chief executive at the helm for seventeen years, the major Hyechka event was an annual May Festival and Concert, first presented in 1907. The show featured local musical talent to enthusiastic audiences, but occasionally the affair showcased well-known national and international artists. In 1912 Clinton became the first president of a local chapter of the Daughters of the American Revolution. That year, also, meeting in the First Presbyterian Church, Clinton and cohorts formed the Council of Women. Two years later she used her ability and civic-mindedness to establish the Philharmonic Society.

For nightly family entertainment, the Dreamland Theater offered productions that traveling thespians of sometimes questionable talent performed. The management was first to show a moving picture, "The Gay Deceiver," on June 7, 1906. The Lyric Theater challenged the original movie house in February of 1908, advertising that it was "the first motion picture theater in the state to present two complete reels every day."

The apex of popular entertainment was the Grand Opera House, which George E. Johnson built. He opened it on February 1, 1906 and did not close it for almost thirty-five years. "The Chaperon" played the first night, and throughout the decades the establishment billed such nationally renowned performers as "the famous funny fellows, Wook and Wand," in the "jolly jungling musical farce, 'Two Merry Tramps.' " Serving a dual capacity as playhouse and public meeting center, the hall constantly echoed with music, speeches, and frivolity. People came to view vaudeville shows and to discuss public controversies. The establishment even withstood competition from the Theatorium, which opened the year after Glenn Pool and featured "Edison's moving pictures."

Other individuals in Tulsa who made things happen included attorney Harry Campbell, who in 1895 moved to Tulsa from Hamilton, Illinois, by way of Pawnee, Indian Territory, driving a team of mules and carrying a one-book law library. Friends called him "judge" although he never held judicial office, and his law practice suffered for a few years until he received a modicum of fame by drafting the petition of incorporation. His sense of civic responsibility never waned, however, and he remained active and influential in the state Democratic Party until his death, in 1950. A man who had seemingly unlimited energy and ambition, he participated in the spectacular chamber projects and served as a director of the Oklahoma Historical Society for twenty-five years. Attorney James Hall once praised him by saying that when he [Hall] died he "would trust Harry Campbell with my whole estate, because Campbell would wind it up to the best interest of my family."

Joining Campbell was his close professional and personal friend, Judge L. M. Poe, who came to Tulsa from Pawnee the same year as Campbell. He served one term as Tulsa's second mayor and another as state district judge after Oklahoma entered the Union. A booster from the time he arrived, he labored hard for the chamber and, after he stepped down from the bench, as chief counsel for the First National Bank.

Despite the fact that Tulsans often felt obliged to work together, the city was highly partisan. The majority of citizens in Indian Territory favored the Democratic Party. The Republicans, however, had an especially strong following in Tulsa. Whenever the Tulsa Republicans and Democrats agreed upon a common goal, such as the Spavinaw Water Project, government could be highly efficient. The commotion over lawlessness, however, represented an exception, for no matter how much either political faction claimed to be against it, no one could or would completely clean up the town.

People associated with the oil industry often resembled the stereotypical cowboy and enjoyed strong drink, a high-stakes poker game, a good fight, or a prostitute's company. Consequently Tulsa was an "open town," and plenty of saloons existed south of Main, in which a person could buy a wide variety of diversions. Each political campaign brought cleanup promises. Candidates from both camps supported virtue, while the chamber admonished people that new industries would not emerge for fear of lawlessness. City officeholders, however, appeared to make only weak attempts to crack down on vice. Those who worked behind the scenes to keep brothels in operation argued that "victimless crimes" would always exist because certain sorts of people would always demand the services; if Tulsa was to hold oil men's attention, they argued, the town had to remain open. John A. Oliphant, one of Tulsa's first police chiefs, observed that "there were a good many men–oil prospectors for the most part–living rather careless domestic lives. . . ." One male might have a "number of housekeepers, cooks, and laundresses" living with him; moreover, the "conduct . . . was flagrantly bold," he charged. Moralistic *World* articles heralded that "Tulsa . . . puts to shame the rotten days of ancient Rome." Apparently the paper voiced what many helpless citizens believed was happening to their city.

The failure to act stemmed from two sources. The first was that a continual population explosion created shifting political sands, thereby offering neither candidate nor officeholder a dependable constituency. L. J. Martin, a Democratic mayor from 1910 to 1912, believed that he served "the people" when he personally led gambling house raids, but he left office virtually friendless because of his actions. Certainly no politician wanted to test mercurial waters by making an honest attempt to change the town, if defeat was to be his or her reward. The second was that many of the reformers were not so well organized as were their fellow progressives in other Oklahoma towns or throughout the nation. For instance, local temperance meetings conspicuously drew scant attendance and financial support.

Another general cause for political ineffectiveness began during territorial days with the caucus system, under which both political parties operated until statehood. Every even-numbered year, in February, this process of electing city functionaries began at the ward level. There party officeholders chose delegates to the county convention at which delegates nominated candidates for various public offices. Progressives from both camps charged that the system was undemocratic because the nominees did not always reflect public opinion. To this charge the bosses rejoined that ward meetings were open to the people and, in addition, party powers did not believe that their models (political machines such as Tammany Hall in New York City) were evil–only efficient.

The door to more responsive government opened in 1908 with the new city charter (to which we have referred earlier). A popular election in each ward produced two spokespersons to participate in a revision that reflected Progressive-Era thinking. Among other results relating to education and rezoning, the document made utility rates subject to city regulation. To make the government more responsive to public opinion, the drafters included local initiative and referendum so that citizens could originate and pass laws. The most novel proposal was the mayor-commission government in which all the public servants had to run for election as at-large candidates. Galveston, Texas, was the first city to try such a plan, and its popularity had spread throughout the nation. The charter came before the people in a special election held on July 3, 1908, and passed by a vote of 992 to 636. Governor Haskell's signature, on January 7, 1909, made the new Tulsa government the first of its kind in the state.

Noble as progressivism was, unfortunately for minority Americans the movement did not address their problems. Concerned whites and blacks did form the National Association for the Advancement of Colored People, in 1909, as the drive to eliminate racial discrimination came throughout the country, primarily from outside most progressive political platforms. In Tulsa one found few exceptions. Throughout the early 1900s black migrants had continually joined the descendants of Indian Territorial slaves in Tulsa. The entire group settled along First Street between Madison and Lansing avenues in the formerly mentioned Greenwood District, a strip of land on Greenwood Avenue. In 1905 the city council sold parts of the site to various black inhabitants. A few had acquired enough capital to open small shops. Owen W. Gulky, a grocer, and Thomas Gentry, a real estate owner, were two of the first business people. By 1910 other entrepreneurs had joined embryonic black capitalist ventures in Tulsa and some made large profits from small initial investments.

Many whites and Indians alike began worrying about the political power that blacks might exercise in local matters. Thus the 1908 city charter made Tulsa the first Oklahoma town to legalize Jim Crow laws and a grandfather clause, preventing segments of the black population from voting and segregating education, as formerly mentioned; moreover, city personnel conscientiously enforced the prohibitions. The question of black power overshadowed other issues in the national and local elections of 1912. Each political party tried to "outrace" the other in a desperate attempt to "blackbait." Accounts of Negro crime, murder, and brutality appeared on a daily basis in the local press. Democrats promised that if voters supported their Southern-oriented philosophy, "Tulsa shall not be dominated by niggers as it will be with the Republican party in control." The enfranchised speculated openly about enacting racial population quotas. When three Negro families moved from Muskogee, the *Tulsa Daily Democrat* warned, "Tulsa appears now to be in danger of losing its prestige [sic] as the 'whitest' town in Oklahoma."

Other communities in Oklahoma and the South shared many Anglo Tulsans' fears. On June 26, 1912, Broken Bow whites attacked the black section of that town, and when the battle was over 200 men of both races lay dead or seriously injured. A few years later, riots broke out in St. Louis, Missouri; Houston, Texas; and Chicago, Illinois. People stood in bewilderment while homes disintegrated into ashes and fellow Americans killed one another;

Collage of Tulsa business buildings and hotels, 1914. Pioneer Hotel is actually the Pioneer Telephone Building. (*Courtesy of the Beryl Ford Collection, Tulsa, Oklahoma*)

Reeder Building and Hotel, northeast corner of Second and Boston, Tulsa, 1912. (*Courtesy of the Beryl Ford Collection, Tulsa, Oklahoma*)

the nation appeared to be on the verge of a second civil war. Although Tulsa survived the Progressive Era with only smoldering racial tension, hot coals remained for the next decades' bugbears to ignite.

The statehood era fomented a cauldron of other partisan disputes throughout Oklahoma. The state convention held in Guthrie, Oklahoma witnessed a dramatic shift from territorial days, because Democratic delegates vastly outnumbered Republicans. President Theodore Roosevelt unwittingly aided his party's Oklahoma antagonists by making himself look like an authoritarian. When the largely Democratic constitution drafters presented their work in Washington, D.C., the President threatened to exercise his veto. Roosevelt was furious because Oklahoma Democrats had accused political enemies of trying to block the statehood drive. When the President finally signed he claimed he could not speak his opinion of the entire affair, because "it was not fit for publication."

Tulsa was also a battleground for the two rivals. The Democrats branded their opponents as the puppets of railroads, insurance companies, and large corporations "who used the people's money to keep the Republican Party in power." In turn, the GOP accused its adversaries of being a coalition of opportunists who bred irresponsibility and William Jennings Bryanism by confusing the voters with nonsensical rhetoric. The elitist stigma haunted the Tulsa Republicans, and in 1908 Democrats won the vast majority of city elections, although a Republican, John O. Mitchell, did become mayor. The Democrats grasped the chief executive position in 1910, placing Commercial Club advocate and longtime booster L. J. Martin over H. O. McClure. The GOP lost again until 1916 when its foes suffered from accusations of corruption during Mayor Frank Wooden's administration. A special city records audit revealed that Democrats had used the people's money to pay party expenditures; thus Republicans, running on a law-and-order platform, soundly defeated the opposition that spring.

Although political competition remained fierce, interest groups shared the ultimate goal of making Tulsa a showplace. Boosters moved in and out of government service, and by 1920 an agrarian society of Indians and cattlemen had given way to one of white-collar workers. The oil industry attracted large numbers of real estate brokers, finance managers, geologists, engineers, and lawyers, not to mention all the other professionals in fields like education that the bustling city attracted. Even the first oil prospectors soon lost their hold as heirs of the new civilization in the Southwest. Although petroleum and technology had reshaped the landscape and made the local economic system more complex, the goals of new Tulsans differed little, if at all, from those of the first pioneers, for most of them still believed their city to be part of the American West, the land of opportunity.

V

Conflict Paves the Way for Consensus

On the eve of President Woodrow Wilson's second inauguration, many Tulsans, like their fellow citizens around the nation, exuded a confidence similar to that which had thrust their ancestors from being a small, insignificant confederation of English colonies to a country of international prestige and power. Through its conquering of North America the United States finally had completed its "manifest destiny" and stood before the world as the product of Western democracy and free enterprise. Anyone either within the States or abroad who espoused other philosophies was the "enemy" for many true believers. World War I was, as Wilson phrased it, a crusade "to make the world safe for democracy." No community's citizens believed those words more than Tulsa leaders, and their slogan, "Tulsa Spirit," became a commitment to prove their dedication. During the fighting and throughout the 1920s, city events accentuated the white, middle-class, conservative origins of progressivism. The results from 1916 to 1929 were bountiful support of the Allies, interracial violence, allegiance to rightist political candidates offering an environment within which the individual could prosper, and completion of business or city-service projects that made Tulsa a pinnacle of oil power in the country.

During Wilson's first administration the president of Mexico, Victoriano Huerta, was the primary enemy of freedom. Wilson refused to recognize the Huerta government because the old revolutionary had achieved power, in 1912, by assassinating his predecessor, Francisco Madero. For this Wilson decided that he should be punished with economic embargoes, diplomatic and military harassment, and an outright invasion at Vera Cruz in 1914. The situation became so acerbic that the Congress passed the National Defense Act, on June 3, 1916, enlarging the regular army by integrating National Guard units into the active military.

Tulsans patriotically answered the call. Colonel Roy Hoffman of the First Oklahoma Infantry began the formal count. Alva J. Niles, former Adjutant General of the Oklahoma National Guard, veteran of the Spanish-American War, and prominent Tulsa banker, inducted forty-five men into the military. Within a week after this first meeting, volunteers filled the town's quota of sixty-five, and newly formed Company C began training at Fort Sill, Oklahoma. It embarked on July 19, 1916 and arrived in Brownsville, Texas two days later. Instructed as an ambulance unit, it remained on the Rio Grande for six and one-half months under the leadership of General John Pershing. The unit ended its tour of duty on March 1, 1917, returned to Fort Sill and was discharged.

While tensions gradually subsided between the United States and Mexico, they flared between Washington and the central powers of Germany, Austria-Hungary, and Turkey. Wilson and other Americans' disgust with submarine warfare directed him into asking Congress for a declaration of war, on April 2, 1917. Thirty days after lawmakers approved, the men of Tulsa's Company C reorganized as part of the Forty-Second Infantry, Thirty-Sixth Division of the Oklahoma National Guard. Hector G. Lareau took command of the ambulance company in August and, after a six-month delay, led his troops to Fort Sam Houston, Texas, where they drilled. In March the outfit returned to Tulsa but soon traveled to Hoboken, New Jersey. On October 18, it departed for Europe aboard the *U.S.S. President Lincoln* (formerly a freighter in the German merchant marine). The trip proved to be uneventful, and the soldiers arrived safe at Sainte Nazaire, Loire Infèrieure, France, on October 31, 1917. By February of 1918 they headquartered at a small farmhouse known as Maison de Brigue, on the road between Luneville and Saint Clement, part of the Baccarat sector of the front. During heavy fighting Lloyd Beach became the first Tulsan wounded; two others, Herbert B. Baber and Berford Pyle, rushed him to the company hospital, saved his life and earned letters of commendation.

In late spring Company C joined the Fourth French Army at Champagne, from which the Allied command expected the German army to push toward Paris. There, from the fourteenth to the eighteenth of July, it faced ghastly fighting. The Tulsa Ambulance Company carried more than 2,205 men to hospitals during the engagement which military reports described as so fierce that the flash from exploding shells produced sufficient light for men ten miles behind the lines to read newspapers. The thunder was of such magnitude that it echoed in Paris, more than 100 miles away. Disengagement from Champagne gave little time to regroup. On July 24, Tulsans were again in the thick of war at Chateau-Thièrry, a battle fought intermittently until August 6.

After the succession of such heavy engagements, the Tulsans rested at Rozières and Remois for two weeks before joining the 165th Infantry at Haumont, in an embattled sector northwest of Toul. A long-dreaded German offensive began soon thereafter, and the warriors entered a life-and-death struggle at the battles of Verdun and Meuse-Argonne. Company C transported 5,460 men to the back lines during the struggle until November 11, 1918, on which date the retreating German army surrendered. Tulsans served as part of the occupying troops until April 17, 1919, when they boarded the *Mt. Vernon* and sailed home. They arrived in New York on April 25 and at 8:00 P.M. on May 16 paraded down Main Street in Tulsa to Convention Hall. Five thousand people jammed into the area, cheering with joy as their conquering heroes returned.

Other Tulsans had participated in the overseas struggle. The 328th Infantry had fought with the 179th Brigade of the famous 90th Division in the most decisive battles of the war before returning home on June 12, 1918; moreover, Tulsa University and chamber of commerce members organized D Company, 2nd Battalion of the 111th Engineers, which won undying fame during the Saint Mihiel offensive of September, 1918 in the Argonne forest by constructing bridges and roads for the Allied armies.

Citizens who had remained at home showed no less enthusiasm

for the national effort. As early as April of 1916 the chamber mailed a resolution to Congress urging legislators to appropriate whatever funds were needed for preparedness. Once hostilities began, locals immediately organized a Tulsa Council of National Defense and elected as its president, J. Burr Gibbons, the general manager of the Hofstra Manufacturing Company and national director of the Navy League of the United States. Gibbons divided his organization into two parts: an Investigation Department that ferreted out draft evaders, dissidents, or bond slackers; and a Legal Advisory Committee that probed cases of "military slackers" and protected soldiers' families from financial problems. By 1919 the former had found eighty-four cases of disloyalty, caught twelve deserters, and made twenty unpaid Liberty Bond holders "see the light."

Support for "Americanism" involved more than extra-legal citizens' groups, for it required supplying manpower for local military units held in reserve. Under the leadership of L. J. F. Rooney, the Tulsa County Home Guard, consisting of several hundred males, combatted "duplicity and treachery at home. . . ." They "protected" oil fields or airports and maintained a force at a local detention camp, forcing vagrants and "idlers" to work in munitions factories. Home Guard representatives carried firearms and trained at the Tulsa Rifle Club. They took their training quite seriously and believed themselves to be the last line of defense if the central powers should invade the United States, or if internal "revolutionary forces" should attempt to take advantage of the nation's weakened position. The loyalists proved to be brutally efficient, and Tulsa received acclaim as one of the nation's most "patriotic cities."

The men of the Tulsa County Council of Defense also sponsored "victory choruses" or community sings. Beginning at 7:30 every Saturday night the city police stopped public traffic in the downtown area, while local and national dignitaries gave speeches for the war effort and against "anti-Americanism." Children distributed hundreds of thousands of pamphlets containing "Liberty Songs," and Tulsans crowded onto Main Street raising their voices in patriotic fervor. Here the council sold federally issued Liberty Loan Bonds to help finance the war. The government suggested for each participating city a quota based on a community's population. During the first national drive federal officials set Tulsa's quota at $3,566,700, and a joint chamber and council promotional

Tulsa Ambulance Company at Camp Mills, Long Island, New York, October 1917. (*Courtesy of the Beryl Ford Collection, Tulsa, Oklahoma*)

Tulsa Ambulance Company in Neugnahr, Germany, 1919. (*Courtesy of the Beryl Ford Collection, Tulsa, Oklahoma*)

reaped more than $5 million. More than half of the sales were to thousands who purchased low-denomination certificates, but several large firms, such as the Cosden Oil Company, contributed as much as $500,000 each. The second push began slowly. As wartime-inflated prices attacked pocketbooks, people became reluctant to spend. It seemed for a while that the city would fall short of its goal until, once again, a chamber-inspired strategem came to the rescue. Ralph Woods, a local businessman, parked on Main Street a truck containing a large roulette wheel and sold $150 chances to spin a lucky number to win a free bond. The plan was successful, for by the war's end Tulsans had contributed $34,888,510, more than 20 percent of all United States securities sold in the state, and had raised the most money per capita of any town in the nation.

The intense fervor had a destructive side, also, which aroused strong hatred and distrust of people and political ideas that did not seem to coincide with "the right beliefs." Tulsa fanatics were quick to condemn persons of foreign stock who retained sympathetic feelings for their native land (especially Germans). Strong editorials denouncing all types of "unpatriotic" activities appeared almost daily in the major newspapers, fueling the flames of political hatred. Commenting on the random attacks against the nation's German immigrants the *World* stated, "Mob law is deplorable at any time, but in the fever or heat of a desperate war we cannot expect people to listen to reason."

Such attitudes spawned an oppressive social climate in Oklahoma. As observed in its operations, the Home Guard interpreted anything short of flag-waving as potential treason. *Democrat* editors condemned pacifists for harboring pro-German sentiment, and *World* reporters stated, ". . . we are slow to condemn American people of any sort as traitors, but there are many who are giving aid and comfort to our enemies under the plea of liberty of conscience and freedom of speech." Counteraction against subterfuge became an all-consuming passion for numerous citizen groups. Hoping to prevent pacifists and unionizers from influencing locals, the chamber passed, by a large majority vote, a resolution creating the General Censor Board to "recommend or disapprove the various subscription papers being circulated within this community."

Tulsa's rapid industrialization had brought hundreds of semi- or non-skilled workers to town, thus creating in some minds a dangerous social element. During World War I anti-foreign sentiment targeted collective-minded proletariats as the most dangerous enemy of individualism and free enterprise. Especially to the business community, unions exemplified the "organized oppression" of free laboring men, not associations through which a person could express dissatisfaction with the employer. A few months prior to the outbreak of the war, various Tulsa department store blue- and pink-collar employees attempted to unionize clerks and stock boys. Declaring that they stood for an open shop, the Chamber staged a well-organized offensive and temporarily blocked adversaries' efforts. Business representatives noted that the alleged rabble-rousers came predominantly from Eastern European and German stock, proving to the capitalists that collective bargaining meant "Bolshevism." Fanning the fire, Tulsa roughnecks refused to denounce the International Workers of the World (IWW), oil-field men who openly denounced American entry into World War I as blatant imperialism. During the overseas fighting many Tulsans perceived the IWW in particular, and labor in general, as sympathizing with the Central Powers and even with a fellow ally, the recently constructed Soviet Union. Consequently a dissenting proletariat often wore the label "fellow traveler."

Matters came to a head in January of 1920 when United States Attorney General A. Mitchell Palmer ordered mass arrests of labor "agitators" and destruction of meeting halls throughout the country. Conservative Tulsans supported the action and praised Palmer as a protector of liberty; however, extremism served primarily to polarize the city's forces. Tulsa union ringleaders attempted to mobilize hotel and restaurant personnel, while plumbers threatened a strike unless local contractors recognized their right to arbitration. A large cadre of capitalists quickly founded a Citizens' Committee for the Open Shop, which won enthusiastic chamber of commerce support. The owners intransigently halted all construction projects, causing mass unemployment until the opposition relented. Afraid of a jobless future, a sufficient number of plumbers went back to work late in October, breaking the strike. It was a brilliant victory which suppressed liberalism for several years among the Tulsa working class. In the spring of 1921 the chamber proudly reported that a closed shop was conspicuously absent from seventeen printing and seven sheet-metal shops, while 400 carpenters and 300 builders peddled their expertise as independents.

Tulsa conservatives paid victory's prices, for their obsession with individualism spilled over into the other aspects of the city's social fabric. Violence and vigilantism became, for many persons, an appropriate way to settle disputes. The city police department, by either design or lack of manpower, had since frontier days ignored bootleggers, gamblers, and prostitutes. Then a sensationalist crime focused attention on lawlessness. On August 22, 1920 two men and a woman kidnapped taxicab driver Homer Nida, stole his money, took him to Red Fork and shot him in the stomach as he begged for his life. Nida lived until the following morning, long enough to tell his story. Within hours after his death the police arrested three known criminals, Marie Harmon, Roy Belton, and Raymond Sharp. Harmon confessed two days later, and that night a mob stormed the city jail, seized Belton and hanged him. Stopping short of endorsing the frenzied action, Tulsans nevertheless confidently believed such behavior would deter other criminals. The *World* observed, "An incident like that which occurred Saturday night does not take place in a community where law enforcement is a fact and justice both speedy and certain." Governor James B. Robertson convened a grand jury which, after months of testimony, adjourned without indicting any officials, although it condemned the crowd for usurping the law.

To evoke order, more sound-minded people attempted to prevail over those relying on terrorism. In April of 1920 a handful of residents organized a committee of 100 and chose as chairman Herbert D. Mason who immediately set out to investigate the police department's seeming inability to stem the growing tide of anarchy. Before the well meaning could act, the city voted in a new consortium of what also proved to be inefficient officials, unequipped to handle the potentially hostile feelings between persons who appeared to threaten Tulsa's "stability" and many white middle-class zealots.

Augmenting the class clashes, Anglos all over the rest of the nation, as well as in Tulsa, warily observed a growing sense of black anger rooted in the soldiers' experiences during World War I. Many military men found that the service practiced rigid segregation, in both the intermingling of enlisted men and the horizontal movement into the officer corps, although blacks fought just as bravely as did their white brothers and sisters. After the war the brutally inequitable experience combined with blatant discrimination in Tulsa and evolved into a protest against institutional racism. Rather than deal fairly with complaints, many Tulsa whites and Indians merely classed "uppity" blacks with the great horde of other malcontents who challenged the established political and economic authority.

On June 1, 1921 the recently purchased and renamed *Democrat*, the *Tulsa Tribune*, published a short, three-paragraph article entitled "Police Nab Negro for Attacking Girl in an Elevator." The alleged criminal was nineteen-year-old Dick Rowland, and his accuser was Sarah Page, who operated an elevator at the Drexel building and attended a local business college. She charged that in the elevator he had attempted to attack her while en route to the third floor. Within hours after the evening newspaper hit the streets, the long-feared racial confrontation erupted.

At 7:30 that night, Chief of Police John A. Gustafson received a report from City Sheriff William M. McCullough that a rowdy band of whites and a larger group of blacks were gathering outside the county jail in which McCullough held Rowland. Gustafson and his deputies had heard rumors of a possible lynching but believed them to be idle talk. McCullough was not so confident and decided to stay the night with Rowland. McCullough ordered his assistants to run the building's elevator to the top floor and station themselves inside the facility. He then sent a black deputy, Barney Clever, to disperse the growing mob of excited blacks, while McCullough made a similar attempt with the whites. As the two men left the building the crowds met them with jeers and catcalls from both the groups. Each man, however, successfully dispersed his assigned throng. Sheriff McCullough then returned to the jail and met a *World* reporter, who showed him a copy of the telegram that Tulsa Mayor Thaddeus D. Evans had sent Governor Robertson. The message was a plea for help.

Evans's decision came too late. Sometime between 8:30 and 9:00 an anonymous caller phoned a theater in the black community and spread word that whites were going to lynch Rowland. At 10:30 a crowd of black Tulsans twice the size of the first gathered at

First and Cincinnati streets and began trading punches with an even larger force of armed whites. Sporadic firing became incessant as whites determined to drive angry adversaries back into the Greenwood District or what some called "Little Africa," an area twelve blocks wide and two miles long positioned between North Boston and Madison avenues extending from Archer Street northward past Line. The Oklahoma National Guard unit under Colonel Leo J. F. Rooney attempted to separate the warring factions but was unsuccessful. Each side clamored for weapons, and by daybreak looters had vandalized virtually every store and shop carrying guns and ammunition.

The heaviest fighting took place between midnight and dawn on June 1. Blacks made their first stand at Archer Street and Cincinnati Avenue, north of the Frisco track, while a smaller contingent dug in along Sixth Street and Main, on the south side of Standpipe Hill. Snipers, fighting independently, climbed to rooftops north of the track and opened fire on advancing whites. In order to rout out lone gunmen, several white World War I veterans scrambled the heights of neighboring buildings and threw lighted, oil-soaked rags onto the roofs shielding the ambushers. The gusting wind carried the flames, spreading them from one structure to the next, until large portions of the Greenwood District were ablaze. Major fires burned throughout the night and the following day, while smaller ones spasmodically ignited as late as Thursday evening.

White patrols came under fire from blacks along Standpipe Hill, but the advancing force marched in military formation up the incline until the flames became so concentrated that they had to retreat; however, enforcements carrying two machine guns arrived shortly. Daunted, the defenders attempted to withdraw and regroup, only to be caught by opening artillery rounds from two embankments and rifle fire from the left and right. Guardsmen relentlessly peppered bullets into the trapped fugitives for three hours until the survivors, huddled behind trees and shrubs, hoisted a white handkerchief. The guardsmen rushed in, disarming the frightened vanquished, while ambulances arrived on the scene and carried away fifty lifeless bodies, mostly those of young men, women, and children.

The last sizable regiment of blacks occupied the newly constructed Mount Zion Baptist Church. Opponents attempted several assaults against the entrenchments, but to no avail. Finished with the "battle of Standpipe Hill," guardsmen positioned their machine guns and opened fire, while civilians crawled on the ground until they were close enough to set fire to the church. The wooden structure virtually exploded into four walls of flames, threatening to incinerate persons within. Soldiers killed three blacks who rushed from the sanctuary, and, surrendering, the remainder of the force fell to the ground. The last major engagement of the Tulsa race riot was over.

The Guard turned next to restoring law and order. Troops herded refugees into fairgrounds, the National Guard Armory, and the Convention Center detainment centers, where local American Red Cross and other volunteers supplied food, shelter, and medical attention. Newspaper reporters on the scene estimated that more than 3,000 men, women, and children timorously milled inside the encampments while their homes burned, and crazed whites looted their possessions. Guardsmen, determined to halt vandalism, arrested twenty-three men at bayonet point. Governor Robertson dramatically declared martial law, and National Guard Adjutant-General Charles F. Barrett took control of the city government on the morning of June 2. That same day Mayor Evans and Police Commissioner M. Adkinson issued statements ordering all persons back to their homes.

"Little Africa" stood smoldering in the warm summer heat, ravaged as if an alien force had invaded. Far from being outsiders, some of the vandals had even been "special police commissioners" deputized during the night. Inhabitants stumbled over the charred debris and stood grieving by what was all they had left. On the evening of June 2 Governor Robertson was jussively requesting that District Judge Valjean Biddison order a grand jury investigation. That same night, Clever, the black deputy sheriff who had tried in vain to stop the insanity twenty-four hours earlier, sat in his chair inside the county courthouse and openly wept. During the riot he had fought his way home and evacuated a handful of valuables; yet when he returned the next morning all was gone, either burned to a cinder or stolen. Tulsa real estate companies estimated the destroyed property at $2,500,000. The loss of lives was harder to calculate but equally staggering. Newspaper and police reports showed between 30 and 500 deaths, and hundreds

Building afire in northeast section of Tulsa business district during race riot, June 1921. (*Courtesy of the Beryl Ford Collection, Tulsa, Oklahoma*)

National Guard and truck-mounted machine gun enforcing martial law in Tulsa during race riot, June 1921. (*Courtesy of the Beryl Ford Collection, Tulsa, Oklahoma*)

Negroes, captured during race riot, being marched across Second and Main streets to convention hall for pacification, Tulsa, June 1921. (*Courtesy of the Beryl Ford Collection, Tulsa, Oklahoma*)

Devastation from Tulsa's race riot, June 1921. (*Courtesy of the Beryl Ford Collection, Tulsa, Oklahoma*)

suffered injuries sufficient to require hospitalization.

Much to their credit many humane Tulsans immediately began repairing the damage. President Alva J. Niles called a special chamber meeting on June 3. After speeches by General Barrett and other locals, those present elected an executive committee of ten that former Mayor Loyal J. Martin was to head. During the next two weeks he guided relief programs and petitioned help from anyone who would listen. Within two days after the riot the Boston Avenue Methodist Church offered its basement as a center for the wounded and provided temporary food and shelter. Other denominations began drives to collect bedding and clothing for those who had lost everything. Such efforts continued until professional charitable organizations could begin functioning.

Early on the morning of June 2 the Red Cross responded to Mayor Evans's call requesting that it "establish headquarters for all relief work. . . ." With a promise from the Public Welfare Board that it would provide any financing that the agency might need, volunteers opened a general headquarters at the Fourth Street and Cincinnati Avenue Young Men's Christian Association (YMCA) and selected the First Baptist Church as the central receiving station for donations. Physician Paul R. Brown headed the medical team, located at the old Cinnabar Hospital on north Main Street.

Other Tulsans responded with equal dedication. The *Tribune* began a drive for clothing, food, and volunteers and pleaded with citizens to show compassion for those who "will return, not to the homes they had Tuesday afternoon, but to heaps of ashes." The Rotary Club supplied sandwiches and water to 2,000 waifs at the Convention Hall. In an ironic manner the riot was bringing members of both races closer together.

While victims recuperated, authorities began looking for those responsible for the tragedy. The *Tribune* defended whites, claiming that the ". . . uprising has long been in the . . . planning" and describing the white mob that had gathered outside the jail as "largely a curious, good natured crowd." The editors went on to blame the "bad element of niggertown" for fomenting trouble. Attesting to have "reliable information," the *Tribune* further reported that law enforcement people had possessed proof of the paper's accusations but had failed to act on the information. Slow to accept responsibility, the police department ventured the theory that both the IWW and the *Tulsa Star,* a local black newspaper, had preached "so-called equality" and therefore stirred racial unrest.

On June 25 a grand jury under Judge Valjean Biddison handed down its statement that documented the presence of an armed faction of black citizens around the jail as the immediate cause of the turbulence. "There was no mob spirit among the whites [who assembled quietly] . . . until the arrival of armed Negroes . . ." the decision read; however, the jurors blamed only a small coterie of militant blacks whom the tribunal charged with having pressed for equal rights and social equality. "We are glad," the decision read, "to exonerate the great majority of the colored people who neither had knowledge of nor part in either the agitation or the accumulation of arms. . . ." The report went on to note that "Law violations have not been confined to the colored district, [but to] the 'choc' joints, . . . houses of prostitution, and bootlegging [headquarters, which] are more or less common in the city." As the best avenue to avoiding another disturbance the jury recommended that "indiscriminate mingling of white and colored people in dance halls and other places of amusement be positively prohibited. . . ." Despite the segregationist stance, in all probability Rowland never lusted after Page at all, for on June 15, 1921, Tulsa officials released him when the woman declined to testify; moreover, the city of Tulsa officially dismissed all charges against him on September 28, 1921.

Hatred had reared its malignant head and prophetically warned Tulsans that armed conflicts must be stopped lest they further minimize local law enforcement's effect; yet the words fell on deaf ears. Soon the Ku Klux Klan led floggings, and public "tarrings" cropped up all over town. Caleb Ridley, a Baptist preacher formerly arrested for public drunkenness in Atlanta, Georgia, held the first known Tulsa Klan meeting in Convention Hall on August 10, 1921, and by September the local chapter boasted a membership of about 1,500. At first the self-appointed public defenders directed their illegal attacks against suspected criminals whom the local authorities could not, or would not, prosecute. Working at night the Klan abducted its prey, transported him or her out to the countryside, stripped him or her naked and flogged him or her with bullwhips. Although Klan tactics repelled most Tulsans, as long as the offenders operated out of sight, the city ignored them. On April

1, 1922, however, in the middle of the day an estimated 1,700 men in white hoods and flowing robes paraded down Main Street and startled pedestrians. The crowd stood in awe as the formation led by three large men on horseback passed by; the middle man carried an American flag. From time to time individual onlookers cheered and applauded, but the vast majority simply stood in silence. Klan tortures continued during the summer months, but on August 14, 1923, Tulsans reaped the reward for their neglect when Governor John C. Walton declared martial law in Tulsa.

The drastic and unexpected action from the state chief executive's office came, finally, after a daylight flogging of Nate Hantaman, a boardinghouse operator. Tulsa police had taken Hantaman into custody for questioning about possible drug trafficking and then released him. As he walked out of the station two assailants dragged Hantaman into a car and drove him to the outskirts of town. There they bludgeoned and left him naked in a deserted field. Hantaman arduously crawled to a nearby road and flagged down a passing traveler who took him to the nearest hospital. Hantaman's wife telephoned the governor's office, reported the incident and charged the Klan with assault and battery and the Tulsa Police Department with complicity. Walton publicly announced that if Hantaman's assailants were not apprehended within three days he would declare martial law; yet enforcers did not arrest a suspect, and Walton followed through with his threat. That afternoon a contingent of guardsmen under General Baird H. Markham took control of the Tulsa County Sheriff's and the city police commissioner's offices. Within hours Markham issued a declaration establishing a military court impaneled to explore allegations of conspiracy between city servants and the attackers.

Although citizens were shocked by the declaration of martial law, the governor drew strong support from various segments of the community. Recognizing that Walton's attack against crime in the city was in reality an investigation of Klan activities, the *World*, long an opponent of the secret organization, stated that "between the Invisible Empire . . . and the governor, the *World* frankly admits that its choice is . . . Governor Walton." Other media sources throughout the nation also sided with Walton. McAlister Coleman, commentator for *The Nation*, bluntly stated that ". . . the Governor has acted with laudable courage."

With such wide public support Walton felt that he was on stable political ground. On August 31 he ridiculed stubborn Tulsans for not cooperating with the military court, sent 200 more troops and suspended the writ of habeas corpus. In its weekly meeting on Friday, September 1 the chamber decided that although it doubted the guilt of any Tulsa employee, it would abide by the proclamation. To persuade the governor to lift martial law the chamber pledged that Tulsans would clean their own house. By September 15, 1923 the tide of public opinion began turning against Walton and metamorphized into a wave that forced him out of the state capitol. On October 23 of the same year the Oklahoma House of Representatives impeached, and on November 19 the Senate upheld eleven counts against, the chief executive, subsequently removing him from office.

Although legislators found Walton's behavior intolerable, the Tulsa military court plainly illustrated that the Klan frequently practiced terrorism. Jurists even indicted four city men for the flogging of Hantaman, and all had confessed dedication to the Klan. Findings uncovered that the Hantaman beating had not been the only provable offense. In 1922 Klansmen had attacked James Smitherman, known to many as an "honest soul," who registered black voters. His abductors tied him to a tree, whipped him and then amputated his right ear. Such revelations opened the honest people's eyes to the fact that Klan participants were no better than the subversive element that the reactionaries purported to oppose; nor was the Klan a defender of individualism, but only of the collective madness resulting from terrorist logic.

From 1916 to 1928 voters in Tulsa inconsistently bounced from one major political party to the other in search of someone who might insure tranquility. The Democrats won four of the seven mayoral races, but Republicans carried every presidential election except in 1916, when the electorate turned out for President Woodrow Wilson. That year Tulsans marked a split ticket, however, placing GOP challenger James H. Simmons into the top city seat. In 1918 Charles H. Hubbard, an oil driller and staunch Democrat, upset Simmons's bid for reelection, but Hubbard lost in 1920 to Republican Thaddeus D. Evans, a native Iowan and farm loan banker. That year some of the newly enfranchised women helped select Warren G. Harding as president; yet local participants also placed as city auditor Mrs. Frank Seaman, the first female public official.

Pejorative press coverage detailing his right-wing affiliation branded Mayor Evans as incompetent and opened the door for Herman F. Newblock, a man who led Tulsa politics for the next six years. Born in Arkansas, he had moved to Cleveland, Oklahoma while still young and had served as sheriff before migrating to Tulsa in 1908. He quickly entered public service and became sheriff of Tulsa County for six years, while dealing in real estate as a sideline. He served on the city council under mayors Hubbard and Evans; then in 1922 he attained the local top spot on the Democratic ticket.

Longtime Tulsa politicos picked Newblock as the favorite, but the Republicans gave a surprisingly strong challenge. Realizing that Evans could not win reelection, the GOP nominated John R. Hadley, a lawyer and oil executive. A native of Indiana, he had come to Oklahoma in 1912 and moved to Tulsa shortly thereafter. Hadley soon became a major Republican figure who served on the State Central Committee and as a delegate to the Republican National Convention in 1916. His only serious drawback was that he had never stood for an elective office, and Newblock made that weakness a key point. He described himself as a "conservative, deliberate, and steady city planner" (a progressive), while he depicted Hadley as a good, honest man, not capable of leading a metropolis such as Tulsa which was always in a state of transition. Republicans emphasized their candidate's longtime support of the Spavinaw project, but that stance proved to be weak because Newblock had also worked for the program. The GOP's biggest trump card was the insinuation that Newblock quietly favored Klan platitudes and practices, causing the mayor to barely win reelection.

Holding tightly to his job, Newblock even survived the 1924 Calvin Coolidge presidential victory and in 1926 trounced mayoral challenger William B. Weston, an avowed Klan member. Even the Republican oriented *World* failed to support its party's choice, recording only that Weston's "Klan connection and sympathy are an anathema to our beliefs." In 1926 the *Tribune* happily noted that there were 27,648 registered voters in the city and that 16,983 of them were Democrats.

Newblock's downfall came during his fourth term, in 1928, with

Al Smith's presidential bid. Tulsa Republicans picked a strong mayoral candidate, Dan W. Patton, the man who had laid out the original city townsite. The old surveyor implied that Newblock headed a Democratic machine, hammering home the theme of individualism and "democracy, not Ring Rule." The election board's tally sheet documented Newblock's "last hurrah," for Patton defeated him by 2,600 votes. Other Republican candidates swept the city posts, and presidential candidate Smith lost Tulsa by more than a two-to-one majority. The national race did produce one interesting side note, when the *World* and the *Tribune* switched sides. Richard Lloyd Jones, the new *Tribune* owner, had purposely changed the name to a less partisan title. Although Jones called himself a Democrat, party-line comments rarely appeared in his paper, and editorials consistently supported candidates of his conscience. For instance, Jones refused to endorse Al Smith because of his association with New York City machine Tammany Hall. Loyal Tulsa Democrats charged the editor with harboring anti-Catholic sentiment, but Jones angrily retorted that if Smith supporters were going to scream "anti-Catholicism" at those who sincerely disagreed with [the candidate's] proposals, then [it was not he, but] Smith who was the bigot." *Tribune* editorials pictured Republican presidential candidate Herbert Hoover as "the true progressive . . . against government ownership [of property] when it is an end and not a means . . . to equalize prosperity among all classes. . . ." *World* journalists, on the other hand, found much of the Democratic platform to their liking. Smith, the "vet" candidate, favored ending prohibition, "not to open new saloons, . . . but to take alcohol from the criminal element." The *World* portrayed Smith as a courageous man willing to stand on principle and not take a position simply to win votes. Although he may have been brave, Smith proved not to be the Tulsa favorite, for Hoover defeated the "Happy Warrior" by more than two to one.

President Hoover had carried the vote in Tulsa because he fit the definition of "progressive" held by a majority of the polity. Through the political and social turmoil after World War I until Governor Walton's impeachment and conviction in 1923, the old excitement over technological progress never waned. Like citizens throughout the nation, by the twenties many people had forgotten about price fixers and monopolists and concentrated on progress as an end, rather than as a means, for all persons to reap economic rewards. Appropriately, in the International Blue Book of 1921 Clarence B. Douglas announced:

> Tulsa wants 100,000 population in 1922, more good families, more industrial plants, more inter-urban lines, more good farmers for rich agricultural lands, more good stock raisers, more good dairymen, more good gardeners and truck farmers, more good orchardists, more wholesale houses, more department stores, more distributing houses for this trade territory, more railroad commercial agents. . . .

In other words, Tulsans, like men and women everywhere, had become obsessed with the creed of materialism, that "more" is always better, and by 1930 the city's 141,258 inhabitants clamored for it.

Industrialists answered the call. In 1922 William K. Warren founded one of the major petroleum and natural gas firms, the Warren Company. Pioneering in the development and construction of barges for both inland and seagoing commerce, the Warren Company dealt exclusively in fuel on a high-volume basis. It bought gasoline during periods of surplus and stored it in huge tanks until demand rose to profitable levels. By 1930 the Warren Company had grown into one of the largest United States wholesalers, and Warren led Tulsa free enterprise.

At a halfway point in the decade, construction was going on everywhere. In 1925 builders finished the Tulsa Club, a ten-story office building. Not far away, at Fifth Street and Cheyenne Avenue, John D. and Cass A. Mayo completed their five-year project, the Mayo Hotel. They legitimately advertised it as the "finest hotel between the Mississippi River and the West Coast." Two years after the establishment opened, the National Bank of Tulsa directors and oil man Waite Phillips announced within months of each other that each was beginning work on a new skyscraper which they subsequently completed in 1929. The Philtower stood twenty-three stories high and housed numerous executives, and the new National Bank climbed upward twenty-seven stories. Commercial growth was everywhere; in 1928 alone, the city issued $12,696,672 worth of building permits. At the same time that the metropolis was sprouting up, it was also expanding. After several years of debate between citizens of Tulsa and the Red Fork hamlet, the city annexed the old oil rival in the fall of 1927. A few months later the population count stood at 20,000, forcing the residential area north and northeast until Tulsa covered 17.51 square miles. That year workers installed 3,000 electricity meters in new homes.

The transportation system continued developing throughout the decade. During the latter part of the nineteenth century, towns needed railroads to entice commerce; by the 1920s the marketplace in turn demanded more modern transit. The city, in a perpetual state of road construction and repair, rebuilt old dirt and stone streets to accommodate a proliferation of automobiles. That year Tulsans spent $3 million for paving 110,243 square yards of avenues, and a decade later traffic was so heavy that the city installed the first electric signals in the downtown area. Passenger service to and from other towns and cities increased beyond all imagination. In 1927 Tulsa serviced so many rail travelers that the polity voted $1,250,000 in bonds to build a new Union Station.

Aviation was the single greatest transportation boom that came to Tulsa. The airplane was primarily used as a carnival and circus attraction since Orville and Wilbur Wright launched the first successful flight of a motor-driven machine on December 17, 1903. By the beginning of World War I many persons argued that air travel was the wave of the future. Precocious Tulsans were determined to be in on the ground floor of the experiment, and in 1917 the chamber formed an "aviation land site committee" to buy property and construct an airstrip and signal tower. Within two years Duncan A. McIntyre, a seasoned veteran of the barnstorming circuit, owned and operated the city's commercial airport. Located four miles east of town, by 1919 the McIntyre Airport was the second largest in the United States and the only one with runways lighted for night flights and long enough for all two-passenger planes. The airfield earned national acclaim in July of 1919 with the first interstate shipment of goods that left the city, bound for a Kansas City, Missouri factory. The historic Tulsa feat caught the federal government's attention, and in August Henry M. Hickam, director of the National Air Service in Washington, D. C., added Tulsa as a regular stop for all transcontinental mail and military flights.

After the promising start, tours to and from Tulsa slowed during the next seven years because, according to Aviation Committee chairman William Holden, Tulsa needed a better facility which would include "a St. Louis air connection." United States Army major C. H. Biddlecombe met with chamber executives and stressed that if Tulsa could obtain a place on a projected Pan-American route linking North and South America, the city would become a center for the Southwestern airline industry. The chamber immediately began formulating a plan that C. H. Terwilliger spearheaded to raise funds for a site. Not wholely satisfied with the effort, William G. Skelly, Waite Phillips, Harry Rogers, Omar K. Benedict, and Cyrus S. Avery organized the Tulsa Airport Corporation and promised to purchase a tract of land suitable for a major operation, if the city would guarantee reimbursement. Satisfied that they would make a return on their investment, the men selected a spot just south of present-day Mohawk Park and immediately began construction. The first runways were little more than "earthen strips carved out of a wheat field," covered with chat to harden the surface, but Tulsans beamed with pride and invited national dignitaries to the three-day festivities opening Tulsa International Airport on July 3–6, 1928.

City manufacturers took further steps to ensure their position within the aviation industry. For instance, later in 1928 Skelly organized the Spartan Aircraft Company and opened a school of aeronautics to instruct pilots and mechanics, making Tulsa the center for training programs in the Southwest. Now executives from all parts of the world could easily come to observe the latest Tulsa techniques of producing and marketing petroleum.

Tulsans celebrated their technological advancement in 1923 by holding the International Petroleum Exposition; this followed the age-old blueprint for state fairs, trade shows, and commercial exhibitions. The first oil exposé had been held in Dallas, Texas in 1921, and the show attracted such a large number of spectators that Tulsa lawyer Earl Sneed advised business leaders that the event should take place in "the recognized center of the oil industry. . . ." The chamber immediately went to work on Sneed's proposal, appointed an ad hoc committee headed by H. O. McClure, polled local capitalists and oil barons and found them receptive to the project. On hearing McClure's findings, a select group organized the International Petroleum Exposition. Directors Lewis B. Jackson, J. M. Hayner, William A. Vandever, William Holden, and James J. McGraw planned and executed the entire affair.

Tulsa Municipal Airport, northeast corner of Apache Street and Sheridan Avenue, 1928. Airport was eight miles northeast of downtown. (*Courtesy of the Beryl Ford Collection, Tulsa, Oklahoma*)

Activities began on October 2, 1923, and captains of major oil concerns discussed problems and future solutions. The gathering exuded an international atmosphere because foreign representatives and speakers also appeared on the program. The coronation of a "King Petroleum" was a central event, spotlighting a local senior citizen who reigned over the week-long festivities. Understanding that success rested not on how many professionals attended, but on the general public's enthusiasm, the organizers scheduled parades of colorfully decorated floats, high school bands, and military drill teams to delight audiences. Throughout the seven days a carnival of acts, brought from as far away as France, such as the Paris Follies, joined with Finks Comedy Circus, the Six Belfords' trapeze act, and Hollywood headliners to entertain several hundred thousand onlookers from all sections of the United States. A beauty pageant, crowning a young Tulsa girl as Miss Queen Petroleum, culminated the festivities. The extravaganza ended a huge success and thereafter became an annual event.

Throughout the bizarre and beautiful decade of the twenties it seemed that many residents had forgotten bedrock progressive notions that equitable education was a cornerstone for any burgeoning civilization. The average monthly teacher's salary throughout most of the decade was $85, compared to $240 for plumbers, $192 for bricklayers, $180 for painters, $168 for carpenters, and $135 for police. Of these typical skilled blue-collar vocations, only stenographers made less than educators—$80 a month. Although a 1927 hike saw $1,600 for women and $1,900 for men annually, the sum was still comparatively low. In addition the board of education systematically refused the national American Association of University Women's requests to include a female among its ranks; and the entire school system continued to segregate blacks from whites and Indians. (Many of the latter had assimilated quite thoroughly.) Although Tulsans sanctioned a $175,000 bond proposal in 1928, most of the educational inequities remained unchallenged; and even though racism and sexism were common in public schools throughout the nation, Tulsa's general support lagged behind other states of the period that literally poured funds into their learning institutions in the hope that education could make dreams of high status and extreme wealth come true.

In scanning a decade following the Progressive Era beginning

Tulsa skyline at night, from atop the Mayo Hotel, 1928. (*Courtesy of the Beryl Ford Collection, Tulsa, Oklahoma*)

with World War I and extending throughout the twenties, we find that for many Tulsans the urban frontier promise spelled rabid patriotism; and industrialism became a golden calf. Charity did follow the racial upheavals, however, and many persons' disgust over Klan activities proved that not all Tulsans had lost their civic concern; yet the watchword was still preserve prosperity above all else, and appropriately the "Magic Empire" became Tulsa power brokers' new city slogan. Even so, economic forces greater than city entrepreneurs could generate lurked in the wings waiting to decimate visions and breathe life into a sluggish social conscience.

VI

Great Depression Years

The shock of the October 1929 stock-market crash and the ensuing Great Depression did not fully reach Tulsa for two years. Until the winter of 1931 ranchers, dry-goods salesmen, retail store managers, and oil-field workers continued their daily lives. All were thankful that they lived in the Great Plains area of the United States, rather than along the eastern seaboard, where the economy had faltered and people were without jobs. Tulsans boasted of living in the fastest growing and the richest-per-capita city in the world. There were few signs of an approaching depression in 1930. Unemployment statistics were low, and the amazing commercial success story, now thirty years old, had instilled in Tulsans a confidence that their environment would not suffer from the economic collapse. In the winter and spring of 1929–30 the citizens passed two bond issues totaling $6,880,000: the first appropriated funds for major street improvements, more sewers, new parks and playgrounds, additions to the five fire stations, and two new municipal hospitals; the second approved the city government's request to buy tracts of land for a future airport. These would be the last expansion measures of the decade that the Tulsa treasury could generate, for soon would come the firing of public servants and cuts in salaries and city services. In the meantime many people sensed confidence in the air, although oil men and bankers had worried looks on their faces.

The economic climate may have been sunny and warm, but, as some suspected, a storm was brewing in the distance. Despite its colossal achievements in the first three decades of the twentieth century, Tulsa's continued good fortune depended on a set of unstable monetary factors. The city was the unchallenged oil center of the Southwest and the major wholesale outlet for South American and Latin American oil, but capitalists had largely ignored substantial opportunities for developing other industries. Tulsa was a one-industry town, an unhealthful characteristic. The volatile oil-market price compounded the potential danger, making drilling for petroleum a highly speculative business. During periods of prolific production and high demand, oil men had the capital to invest in other local industries but often chose not to do so. Economic expansion in Tulsa during the 1920s therefore was quite irregular.

Cyclical prosperity affected Tulsa's working class which consisted primarily of unskilled and semiskilled oil-field hands; such persons went jobless when production slumped. The copious periods, however, continued to attract large numbers of sojourners, especially former farmers, and by 1930 Tulsa's labor force had expanded beyond the number of available jobs, even in times of peak prosperity. In 1930 the discovery of new pools in Seminole and Oklahoma City, Oklahoma, added to East Texas, drove the price to one cent per barrel. Finally in the winter of that year Tulsa's economy crumbled. Early relief efforts came from private foundations. American Red Cross volunteers operated as they had after the twenties' riot; a natural disaster had struck. They led drives for food and provided free medical facilities for the sick. The local Community Fund established soup lines and "rest houses" for men and their families left destitute by the sudden financial debacle; however, money was never plentiful.

City government officeholders and other interested locals prepared for the disaster by studying what other cities had tried in order to stem the tide, and by fall of 1931 a movement was under way to organize a comprehensive and effectual program for the town and its surrounding area. Tulsa leaders turned to Charles C. Day who had helped design such a plan for Oklahoma City. Speaking before the chamber of commerce, Day advised Tulsans to create one agency responsible for clearing private, church, and governmental efforts to relieve suffering. He emphasized that the merchant and industrial classes must take the leading role, or ". . . we certainly will go under the dole, and then the businessmen who did not act will squawk to high heaven."

Day's words found a receptive audience. The chamber elected a fact-finding committee, which Alfred L. Farmer chaired, to survey and make recommendations as to what the chamber could do to help facilitate rescue operations. During the next thirty days the group issued a questionnaire to all philanthropies, inquiring into each agency's operations and how it could improve. Farmer's subordinates also investigated the Better Business Bureau record, the City Solicitations Committee, and the Community Fund, in addition to considering ideas generated in other communities. When presenting a report to chamber representatives, Farmer stressed that previous remedies had been extremely inefficient because they had duplicated one another; success or failure therefore depended on how cooperative the federal, state, county, and city administrations were. To ensure harmony, Farmer and his cohorts requested that Tulsa officials establish a Central Committee of Five, consisting of one delegate from each of the following–the Community Fund, the chamber, the city administration, county commissioners, and the general public–to direct and oversee Tulsa city and county actions. The Farmer findings went on to say that although the concept of centralized authority was anti-individualistic and therefore might be controversial, only such commandeering could prevent chaos and disaster. H. O. McClure praised the investigators for their brainstorming, and the chamber board of directors voted to sanction the scheme.

Today no one knows just how much bargaining went into persuading the relief agencies to accept the Farmer proposal, but by October 16 the Central Committee, consisting of H. O. McClure, president of the Tulsa Industrial Finance Corporation; Harry Schwartz, president of the Tulsa Labor Council; Ernest Cornelius, president of the Oklahoma Steel Castings Company; major John Leavell, president of the Leavell Coal Company and delegate of the city administration; and municipal judge G. Edward Warren. To consolidate authority they commended successful charitable drives and asked inefficient agencies to discontinue operations. The Central Committee also ordered the Community Fund not to replicate other organizations' programs and told the Social Service Bureau to review each one who applied for money to ensure that he or she had not received funds elsewhere. McClure demanded that handouts be confined to the aged, the infirm, and families without adult male members, saving employment opportunities for those able to work. The Central Committee also combined the unemployment registration lists of the county government with the names of relief applicants registered with the Social Service Bureau so that it could judiciously parcel out jobs.

After one week of existence the Central Committee, reacting to public pressure, set forth a detailed plan to end Tulsa panhandling. Hundreds of men and women, unable to find employment of any sort, had resorted to begging or selling apples, oranges, and rags in the city streets. During the spring months of 1930, before Tulsans really experienced the Depression, fortunate persons took pity on the impoverished and hired them to rake leaves, mow lawns, or perform other household chores in return for food. As the economic situation worsened, however, beggars became a public menace and received less-than-cordial greetings. The Central Committee partially alleviated the problem by establishing community rooming houses for transients and even authorized the city's first overnight home for Negro men; yet the program did not eliminate the human refuse from the industrial orgy of the 1920s.

Frustrated by its only partial success, the Central Committee called on "responsible citizens" to submit thoroughly planned suggestions, of which the body received 100. The proposals, although varying, fell into two major categories–city-financed public works, and more money given directly to needy persons. Somewhat unique among the many drafts was that of Michael C. Hale, a Tulsa hardware dealer. He proposed that the city purchase $40,000 worth of edible commodities at wholesale prices. The Central Committee could supervise the distribution of the foodstuff, rationing daily requirements such as two pounds of potatoes, one pound of sweet potatoes, one loaf of whole-wheat bread, one pound of cornmeal, one pound of salt pork, one-third pound of beans or peas, one quart of skim milk, one-fourth pint of sorghum, and one-fourth pound of lard. The diet was adequate nourishment for four people, and at depressed farm prices the city for $40,000 could buy sufficient food to feed an estimated 2,500 families. One could obtain the groceries through the Federal Farm Board, in cooperation with nearby agrarians. Hale offered to donate a mill and a corn sheller to prepare and store the food, respectively, thereby saving costs.

Two additional plans, one called the Grain Plan and the other the Antle Plan, which Tulsa cattleman Arthur F. Antle introduced, agreed with Hale but elaborated further. The Grain Plan suggested that the city purchase wheat from farmers in western Oklahoma, ship it to local mills to be ground into flour and sell it at a central commissary for a nominal price. The city could procure meat by buying and slaughtering fat hogs under current prices which were so low that farmers were currently killing, rather than selling, the animals. The Antle Plan called for the city to develop a cooperative farm on which the idle might work to feed their families. Tulsa could buy an eighty-acre tract just outside the city, construct a canning factory in the vicinity and distribute the products to those who had produced them. Lodged in conservative tenets, the Central Committee did not adopt any of the collective-oriented propositions, although it did facilitate distribution of charity during 1931.

In September of 1931 Democratic mayor George Watkins announced his administration's scheme. The written proposal began be recalling that the Supreme Court of Oklahoma, in 1929, had invalidated already collected county levies totaling $900,000. The Tulsa treasurer's office had subsequently impounded the funds until the city could return them to the taxpayers. Watkins suggested that, instead of reimbursing the citizenry, Tulsa should hire the destitute to labor on public projects. In the long run the program would mean more to Tulsans than a return of their money, Watkins reasoned. The mayor stated that the first city endeavor would be to construct a reservoir in Mohawk Park and that recreational area improvements would be made in the same manner; the Watkins vision therefore was known as the Mohawk Plan.

The mayor drew direct attack from private citizens, corporations, the federal government, and the Central Committee. Robert Letcher McKee, president of the Tulsa Taxpayers Association, a group that had helped influence the Court to declare the 1929 levy unconstitutional, pointed out that Tulsans had expended thousands of their own dollars already and should not have to make further sacrifices. Representatives of the Public Service Company reminded the mayor that, although the company favored a program that would force recipients to work for government assistance, the city should return the revenue from an illegal tax and allow each individual to voluntarily contribute a portion of his or her refund. Others, representing only themselves, criticized the Mohawk Plan, complaining that the "common man" always bore the tax, but absentee landlord oil companies, which had made millions out of Oklahoma's soil, paid nothing in local levies. Another irate citizen argued that the Mohawk Plan, a make-work program, provided for only families with male heads. "What about the women who are heads of families, or the orphaned children?" she asked. Should not the city take responsibility for those unable to participate?

The Central Committee, although unable to come up with an adequate plot of its own, joined the public assault. It predicted that the city would need more than $1 million in payroll funds for merely twenty weeks, and the impounded funds totaled only $900,000. The Central Committee therefore asked that the city request from the County Excise Board a readjustment of the Tulsa water department's budget, thereby salvaging the additional $100,000 needed to enact the Watkins scenario. The mayor concurred and appealed to the board members, who agreed. At last, in October 1932, the Mohawk Plan went into effect; the Central Committee then turned its attention to those incapable of participating and decided to incorporate a few of the communal notions mentioned in some of the 100 treatises already gathered. Central Committee participant Leavell suggested opening a commissary that would operate as a clearinghouse for meat, grain, vegetables, bedding, clothing, and furniture. Anticipating store owners' arguments that the wholesale operation would unfairly compete with private businesses, Leavell emphasized that the public market would exist only until the depression passed. To reassure the merchants, Central Committee members further promised that they would order all agricultural goods from Tulsa area farmers, make only cash purchases, and supervise all transactions. Despite continued assaults from business people, the Central Committee unanimously adopted the idea.

The experience of World War I had taught us, Leavell stated, that any distribution of goods required that beneficiaries buy through a special ration system. This method would ensure two things–

lower unit costs and provide proper nourishment for indigent persons. Leavell projected, and he was correct, that the average cost of a weekly food portion would be forty-two cents. The sample diet that the Central Committee approved contained 2,800 calories, more than the Massachusetts Institute of Technology had previously determined ample for a normal male.

Once the new warehouse opened it drew the attention of national and international urban rescue teams. Mayor Watkins spoke before the northern states' legislatures and the governor's cabinet about his and the Central Committee's achievements. His confident demeanor and sound answers to interrogation proved so persuasive that Pennsylvania founded a clearinghouse. Meanwhile, letters of inquiry from thirteen nations arrived in Tulsa asking for comprehensive details about the recovery strategies.

Although Tulsa received wide recognition for its innovative efforts, the Central Committee and the city government suffered continuous financial shortages, for there was no federal or state economic aid to bolster them. The winter of 1932 found Tulsans more desperate than in the previous year. When the Mohawk project began, Watkins established a central file of all unemployed persons in the city to which every approved relief agency had access. That list, by February of 1932, contained 11,675 names and was growing daily. Unless help from other sources should arrive soon, the unemployment rate would rise to 38 percent of the populace.

President Herbert Hoover's administration was somewhat unsympathetic and unhelpful. M. C. Williams, southwest regional director for Hoover's unemployment committee, advised Tulsa to forget even a short-run federal public-works package, because people know "it is just a guise for charity, and those who really want to work for whatever they receive resent [it]." Anti-Hoover and anti-Republicanism therefore grew stronger in Tulsa and throughout Oklahoma. A. F. Sweeney, representing Governor Bill Murray's office, remarked that federal authorities were "passing the buck" with their suggestions and that men like Williams were "fifth wheels," out of touch with the severity of the Depression. Despite federal recalcitrance, in May of 1931 city authorities hit upon an idea for obtaining assistance from Hoover's creation, the Reconstruction Finance Corporation (RFC). A total of $1,300,000 in bonds from a referendum in 1930 remained unsold, and Mayor Watkins decided to sell them to the RFC and use the revenue to finance the faltering Mohawk Plan. Unfortunately Robert W. Kelso, the regional RFC representative, gave only nominal support to the idea, and authorities in Washington responded that as the proposal was highly unusual, a great deal of discussion was necessary.

Frustrated, Tulsans turned to the state and requested part of the $500,000 from RFC assistance to Oklahoma. This avenue of approach proved more successful, for in late October Tulsa received $146,000 for projects including Mohawk Park, waterline extensions, and clearing of timber for a new golf course in the park. More than 1,000 heads of families went to work in shifts of 500, and each person earned $2.40 a day for three eight-hour days each week; in addition, Governor Murray allowed the National Guard to organize a kitchen to prepare food and feed these people on the job.

Tulsa Union Depot and overpass, 1932. (*Courtesy of the Beryl Ford Collection, Tulsa, Oklahoma*)

Limited federal aid, however, was insufficient to solve the city's major problems, for in 1932 Tulsa County unemployment had reached 13,000, and many Tulsans blamed Hoover. Ironically, though, the president's greatest fault was his inability to convince people that he was one of them and that he was in control. Although he gave Tulsans the impression that all he would give them were platitudes on the work ethic's financial healing power, by the end of his term Oklahomans had reaped $125,292,945 in federal benefits. The April 1932 Tulsa city elections foretold the impending Republican national disaster. Herman F. Newblock, in a dramatic political resurrection, won the Democratic Party primary over incumbent mayor George Watkins. His general election opposition came from two fronts–a third-party candidate, Charles W. Grimes, and Republican Dan Patton, Newblock's nemesis in the city elections four years previously. Grimes ran on the issue of cutting city taxes, a sound strategy in normal times but one that Newblock effectively countered by showing that the assessments would pay for city services; Patton, it seemed, did not have an issue. The voters showed which they preferred–lower levies or public works–by narrowly electing Newblock. The results were what Richard Lloyd Jones classified as "a scare for the Democrats," but they nevertheless won every local office except sheriff, for which Charles Price escaped the avalanche.

In the late summer of 1932 Mayor Newblock tried to assist Tulsa's benevolent societies and urged city, county, and business employees or owners to contribute a fixed percentage of their incomes to help finance the distribution of food to the hungry. The mayor's plan had little success, as the Depression worsened and engulfed those to whom Newblock appealed for aid. A full-scale attempt was on the way, however, with the election of Democratic president Franklin Delano Roosevelt in the fall of that year.

The presidential election was just as dramatic in Tulsa as it was throughout the rest of the land. *World* editors came out in support of Roosevelt in April, but the *Tribune,* under Jones, found little in his favor. Roosevelt, in Jones's opinion, was the long arm of Tammany Hall reaching out to choke the life from American democracy, a politician short on leadership ability and long on "waffling." Early city returns gave Hoover a slim lead, but in the end Tulsans had voted for Roosevelt by a margin of 22,787 to 15,933.

The rout did not stop at the top of the ticket. Tulsa County went for the Democratic candidate in every statewide race except that for corporation commissioner, by which ex-Governor Walton attempted, but failed, to reenter the public arena. A despondent *Tribune* editor, searching for the silver lining in what he viewed as a black national cloud, predicted that Roosevelt's election might in the long run benefit the country. *World* owner Eugene Lorton continued to support the New Deal, Roosevelt's game plan, and the president appointed him to an international Joint Committee on Finance in 1933, a post he faithfully filled until he deserted Roosevelt five years later.

True to his campaign promises, the chief executive acted quickly and decisively. In May of 1933 he signed the Federal Emergency Relief Administration Act (FERA), which made direct grants to state and local governments to get public projects under way. Where necessary the agency even personally donated dollars and in the two years of its existence catalyzed disbursement of $4 billion, three-fourths from federal and one-fourth from local funds. Tulsans spent their share building the Central Fire Station and financing continued work on Mohawk Park.

In January of 1935 Roosevelt and Congress replaced the FERA with a more comprehensive system, the Works Progress Administration (WPA), and appropriated $4.88 billion for housing, reforestation, relief loans and grants, public health, education, and rural electrification. Unlike the RFC bureaucrats of the Hoover administration, WPA officials eagerly primed the pump. Within three months after WPA money reached Tulsa, federal officials approved twenty-seven Tulsa proposals, and the city received its first benefits on August 1, 1935 in the amount of $2,606,494. Over the next nine months Tulsans spent $432,964.63 in federal money for such diverse projects as repairing sanitary mains in residential districts of White City, Beverly Hills, and Mark Twain; installing new drainage pipes for Harvard Avenue; and paving along Quanah Avenue and the West Tulsa Traffic Way; moreover, when no grant capital was available, Harry Hopkins, the first WPA director, lent it at a nominal interest rate. Tulsa took advantage of the opportunity by borrowing $12,500 and constructing, with WPA labor, the Tulsa Public Health Building at Eighth Street and Peoria Avenue. Coupled with $184,230 in city tax revenues spent for civic improvements, the incoming dollars provided work for 8,000 Tulsans previously unemployed and gave the local economy a lift.

From June through November 1935 retail sales jumped 3.5 percent, and the city let $131,705 worth of building contracts in October, the biggest total since 1929. The Agricultural Adjustment Act of 1933, New Deal legislation to raise farm prices by limiting farm production, worked just as Secretary of Agriculture Henry Wallace had hoped it would. Tulsa area farmers purchased livestock at a record rate, as indicated at the Tulsa Stockyards in October of 1935, as 1,000 head of cattle passed through the pens and hogs sold for $9.10 each, the highest price for swine in fifteen years.

Tulsans repaid Roosevelt by returning Democratic majorities in city, state, and national offices, in 1934 and 1936. Newblock, his hunger for public service finally satisfied, declined to run for a fifth term in 1934 and threw his valuable support to Thomas A. Penney, a pioneer druggist. Penney and the rest of the Democratic slate, cognizant of Roosevelt's popularity, established themselves as the "local agents for the general . . . FDR recovery movement." Consequently, the GOP lost all city races by a two-to-one majority. Two years later Tulsans overwhelmingly voted, in a record turnout of 70,000, for Roosevelt, the "man who saved the nation." The President received 40,948 votes to Alf Landon's 28,294, and local Democrats returned to the city seats of power.

From his record popularity in 1936, the nation's chief executive suffered his first major political reverse in 1937 when he attempted to "pack" the United States Supreme Court with justices who would view New Deal agencies as constitutional and balance the federal budget by limiting WPA appropriations. The result was a national economic recession, which Tulsans also experienced. The local list of unemployed climbed from 3,886 in January of 1936 to 6,064 by November 1937, approximately 4 percent of Oklahoma's total. A few federal programs remained, such as the Federal Writers' Project which paid a small cadre of Oklahoma educators to write an Oklahoma history and one of Tulsa; yet endeavors were too specialized to employ many people.

The Roosevelt administration did supplement Tulsa public schools during the late thirties. Hard times had forced the system into retrenchment during the early Depression days. The district was burdened with extra costs because of its annexation of Turley and part of Sand Springs suburbs and the increased demand of classes for unemployed youth. Despite hardships, students made social contributions throughout the era by making clothes and participating in WPA gardening and canning projects for the needy; fiscal strain, however, forced schoolboard members to close two elementary schools (Washington and Clinton), cut salaries (especially in the segregated institutions), and eliminate some faculty and administrative positions. Finally in 1937 federal money matched city bond funds and erected two high schools, Webster and Rogers. At the decade's end the people had managed to keep 30,041 matriculants in Tulsa's forty-three schools and elected Mrs. Everett Manning the first female to chair the board of overseers.

The economic relapse continued to press the city's pecuniary foundations. With the number of non-working citizens growing, small firms reneged on mortgage payments and had to close their doors. Business people, faced with prospects of a renewed depression, organized the Tulsa Industrial Corporation (TIC), a finance company to lend money to small firms. Although resources were limited, the TIC prevented a catastrophe, and the city government managed to meet its obligations by cutting public services and collecting $2,008,217 in new taxes. The WPA helped when it could. By October the city's bond indebtedness had decreased from a high in 1932 of $17,429,407 to $13,445,508, a miraculous feat.

The plummeting prosperity fell heaviest on blue-collar wage earners and the majority of the Tulsa minority race. Despite the tragic twenties riot, the number of blacks had increased 15 percent by 1938. Although they remained in subservient roles, after the New Deal had its effect blacks enjoyed pay rates higher than their counterparts in any other Southern or Southwestern city; for instance, Tulsa household servants, porters, and janitors earned ten to twenty dollars a week, but the 1937 setback crumbled the limited gains that many had made. Living conditions in the black community (never good) deteriorated, and social unrest rose. In a July 1938 report to the chamber, John D. Fenaloysen, chairman of the Committee on Public Health and Sanitation, warned that if the city did not provide a health inspector for the black community, collect the garbage, and inaugurate a general cleanup campaign, Tulsa might experience a possible second "uprising." Officials averted the crisis by diverting portions of the remaining WPA funds to improving conditions so that life in the Greenwood District was tolerable.

Tulsa oil-field workers presented authorities with a more difficult problem. Roosevelt knew that the Depression was a fertile ground for labor dissatisfaction, and national leaders had narrowly averted massive labor strikes on two occasions during his first term. By 1938, however, the government no longer was able to stem the tide. Strikes flared throughout the country, and the Tulsa Mid-Continent Oil Company walkout was one of the longest in history. Unrest fomented because owners could not meet their payrolls, and executives were forced to fire a sizable number of employees and reduce wages among those who remained. Job uncertainty created an atmosphere of distrust, which eventually led field workers to request establishment of arbitration machinery to settle disputes. When management refused to discuss grievances and blamed the tensions on "outside agitators," the oil fielders struck on December 22, 1938. Picket lines formed outside refinery gates and remained until the Oklahoma National Guard reached the scene and ordered the men to move three blocks away from the plant entrance. There, for the next sixty-five weeks, protesters armed with wooden signs signifying their demands marched twenty-four hours daily.

The first seven days passed uneventfully; then an unidentified saboteur dynamited a pipeline near Kiefer, Oklahoma. Union leadership denied any complicity, but townspeople's hostility bubbled. Residents harassed children of oil-field personnel, and fights between Tulsans who took sides broke out in the downtown area. Governor Ernest W. Marland dispatched his secretary Rowe Cook to preside over the arbitration conferences at the Mayo Hotel. J. C. Denton, vice-president, general counsel, and spokesman for the Mid-Continent Petroleum Corporation announced that all who had walked out were fired and that the company was hiring new employees. Shocked and disheartened by the drastic measure, Jack Hays, president of the Tulsa local of Oil Workers International and primary negotiator for the union, announced the existence of a battleground that was merely one setting in the worldwide class war, and he concluded that his men would stop any scabs from interfering.

Workers relied on their organization for succor. Community dining rooms at union halls served free hot meals, and families pooled food, clothing, and other necessary resources. Every day representatives of both parties met and negotiated until March 22, 1939, at which time the two sides reached a tentative settlement. The field workers agreed to end the strike, and management promised to exact no reprisals against dissident employees; in addition, if labor showed its good faith, Mid-Continent spokespeople said they would create an arbitration board for settling future conflicts. Neither side declared the agreement a victory, but at least men could again earn wages, and the company could start producing refined oil.

Unemployment declined by 11 percent during 1939 and the first six months of 1940; crowds of eager customers filled the department stores along Main Street. The local Sears establishment broke the company's national record for monthly sales in March of 1940, and the total payroll for all retail distributors reached $9,244,000, the highest aggregate figure in ten years. The revival signs were tempered somewhat by a lagging agricultural market. Farmers and ranchers saw the number of cattle passing through the Tulsa Stockyard's sale ring decline to half the number processed in 1935, a peak Depression year, and the price of hogs descended to $5.15; also, 1,600 men still were working on WPA jobs, and by January of the new decade total revenue on hand amounted to less than $1,000. Beverly Gouldilock, assistant director for the state WPA, announced to the Tulsa chamber that, by order of the president, after July 15, 1940 she was not just cutting but curtailing her agency's programs. The news sent shudders throughout the community. People working sixteen hours a day just to earn enough to buy a few ounces of meat and four pounds of potatoes a week found themselves once again with nothing. The jobless returned to park benches, with elbows on their knees, staring at passersby. The Depression was nine years old in Tulsa, and for some people it seemed like a lifetime that would never end.

The city government reacted as if officials had lost any belief that they could solve or even ease the crisis. The notion that Tulsa, state, or federal government personnel could spend the nation out of the Depression was rapidly losing followers. Mayor Penney had won reelection in 1938 on a platform of cutting taxes, and nothing moved him or the city council from this pledge. Although fiscal stringency did not end, local support for Democratic officials was waning. Tulsans no longer saw Roosevelt as their savior and the New Deal as holy scripture. Democrat Charles H. Veale defeated Republican Lee Pollack for mayor in 1940, but that election was held in April, before the nation's policy makers announced the WPA death; if the Democrats had been forced to run with the President in November, the outcome might have been different. By the fall of 1940, a presidential campaign year, the once friendly *World* blasted Roosevelt for desiring a third term, and owner Lorton published editorials against the policy he once had helped formulate, exclaiming, "The New Deal must be stopped." The nation may not have agreed, but Tulsans turned out in record numbers and gave Wendell Wilkie a 7,000-vote majority. Local Republicans had something to cheer about for the first time in twelve years.

The repudiation of the New Deal was a fruitless reaction against local conditions, and community leaders found that they could do little other than what the federal Democratic moguls had tried. The Tulsa County Commissioners revived the old food-stamp program used in 1933 for low-income groups, unemployed WPA workers, the physically handicapped, and the aged, although city authorities refused to appropriate sufficient funds for its survival beyond six months. State law further prohibited county functionaries, such as Lincoln Salle, from raising money through private donations, although he did manage to finance the program by begging a reluctant chamber for a small stipend and by borrowing $25,000 from the State Welfare Commission, a loan repayable in ninety days. The effort was like placing a bandaid over a gunshot wound.

Fortunately for many Tulsa Depression and recession victims, housing was one area that both federal and local officials consistently supported throughout the thirties. As the suffering had heightened, bankrupt and sand-blown farmers turned to urban centers for job opportunities in a move that increased unemployment in Tulsa. There they found nothing, and their plight had become so acute by 1935 that the Public Works Administration (PWA) allotted $2,000,000 to Tulsa for erection of low-cost housing. The buildings were one-story family units of four rooms each: a bedroom, a bathroom, a kitchen, and a living room; construction, however, could not keep pace with demand.

The federal government replaced the PWA assistance with the Federal Home Administration (FHA) aid in 1940 and soon outlined plans to create residences costing less than $2,500. The new agency proved to be more efficient and more responsive to Tulsa's needs, although conservatives were skeptical of more federal programs. Wade Whiteside, co-chairman of the Civic Engineering Department, campaigned hard for FHA money and worked to convince local authorities that if Tulsa were to be a business and industrial center "we must build homes for people who earn approximately $1,750 a year." In his July report to the chamber, Clyde C. Ingle, president of the Real Estate Board of Tulsa, reinforced Whiteside's message. "The housing problem has reached a crisis stage," said Ingle. "Only 1.9 percent of the residential buildings in Tulsa are vacant, and the single largest complaint from people leaving the city is the lack of shelter." Fortunately, he reported, construction was moving, for 304 low-cost homes were under construction, and 177 new ones were ready for sale. Although the situation did improve, it remained unsolved until American entry into World War II.

Tulsans began discussing the possibility of war in the summer of 1940. If the United States should enter the international conflict already burning in Europe, speculative Tulsans wanted to expand their ability to attract related industries by improving the air-transport facilities. The argument was not whether or not Tulsa should expand, but whether or not improving the municipal airport runways and hangar capacity would be sufficient. Russell Hunt of the chamber Aviation Committee presented his ideas to business people, the mayor, and the city council. In his presentation he used automobile production as an example of what had occurred after World War I. Hunt declared that air travel would be greater after the war than during it and that those cities with modern facilities would make a great deal of money. To prove his point, Hunt noted that air freight had doubled in the past fifteen years and that with American factories gearing to save the allied powers air cargo was increasing. "The Municipal Airport, even after its current expansion is completed, will be congested by the air traffic," the Aviation Committee report concluded.

Additional support for building a new airfield came from a variety of sources. Gill Robb Wilson, president of the National Aeronautics Association, wrote to the chamber in September of 1941, "It is my studied judgment that Tulsa should take steps to acquire the land for a second major air port. . . ." Joining Hunt, Lieutenant Colonel Lucius D. Clay, assistant to the administrator of the Civil Aeronautics Administration, told the chamber that "an additional airport in Tulsa would be of immediate value to the city. . . ."

Those opposing innovation rallied behind recently elected Mayor Veale, arguing that construction of another facility would be too expensive and wasteful. The logical recourse was to expand Municipal Field by extending the length of the runways and building more hangars. Newspaper boys' clarion calls announcing the Japanese attack on Pearl Harbor on December 7, 1941 drowned out Veale faction words. Thirty-nine days after the tragedy, Tulsans, swept up in the national trauma and sense of urgency, voted a $100,000 bond issue for acquiring one section of land for a new airport and renovating Municipal Field. The ten-year struggle against the Depression was forgotten; Tulsans now prepared for war.

Gone was an era of despair in which many Tulsans had temporarily put aside their 1920s preoccupation with the enemies of individualism and resurrected the progressive spirit that had built a city of fellow citizens out of a watering hole or whistle stop on the plains. By the late thirties and early forties, however, many Tulsa leaders tired of merely trying to sustain a faltering economy. They lusted for the environment and the markets that provided the old vision of unlimited vistas for industrial and commercial growth.

VII

Challenge and Victory: World War II to 1960

The era beginning with World War II and ending with the election of John F. Kennedy as President of the United States was filled with challenges; for Tulsa, gearing up industrial machinery and handling late-forties inflation were only two of these. Most residents avidly supported the Allies against the Axis powers, Germany, Japan, and Italy, because the conflict had given them a feeling of unity and the chance to reach for prosperity once again. Oklahoma supplied 144,533 men and women to the front lines, in addition to 60,000 enlistments in the Naval Reserve and 7,500 in the Marine Corps; of these, more than 6,000 came from Tulsa. A combination of loyalty and opportunism spurred the Tulsa business community to launch feverish quests for defense contracts and to establish other war-related industries, which stimulated local corporate profits and fostered numerous white- and blue-collar jobs. The chamber of commerce supported President Roosevelt's idea of an arsenal for democracy and dispatched a resolution to Congress requesting that the government cut back on New Deal spending and instead appropriate funds for tanks, airplanes, and servicemen's salaries.

Mayor Veale and the chamber named A. Roy Wiley, a local physician, chairman of the Tulsa Military Affairs Committee and charged him with coaxing military-oriented business and personnel to the city. Wiley acquired a recruiting station under the Selective Service Act, and, contrary to later Hollywood media portrayals of similar outposts, young men of the city did not rush to the doors; the center proved to be important, however, after the United States entered the war in 1941. Wiley also extracted a promise from Governor Leon Phillips to provide an Oklahoma National Guard hospital unit, as long as Tulsa guaranteed suitable facilities. The city lived up to its end of the bargain, when the Fairgrounds Board donated one of its buildings, and the chamber underwrote a $300 remodeling job.

The early success led to overconfidence, and civic leaders almost lost an additional National Guard unit. In July of 1940 Wiley quoted Phillips as saying that the Tulsa armory was a fine place for an aviation unit, and that as soon as Oklahoma should receive word from Washington, D.C. the governor would dispatch troops to Tulsa. In anticipation the city council placed a bond issue before the people to raise $400,000 to improve the fairgrounds and the Municipal Airport. The referendum passed, but Phillips, a mercurial, hot-tempered man, believed that the Tulsans were pressuring him. The state chief executive therefore threatened chamber president Victor F. Barnett, claiming that he might leave the city "high and dry." The incident slowed plans for the unit until after the United States entered the international struggle.

The Phillips affair only accentuated city leaders' growing concern that among the forty-eight states Oklahoma ranked fifteenth in per-capita income, twentieth in population, but only fortieth in federal arms-related money. The unpleasant knowledge motivated the chamber, which voted to make Russell Rhodes a Washington, D.C. lobbyist to obtain government contracts. During the first six months of 1942 chamber secretary Rhodes made three trips to the nation's capital and used as a lure Tulsa's supposed invulnerability to attack, availability of labor, and proximity of the oil fields. The latter ironically proved to be detrimental to his efforts because War Department bureaucrats informed him that "the oil industry had been so well managed that [they] doubted that it would be necessary for the federal government to aid or encourage gasoline manufacturers." Rhodes's numerous attempts to locate a munitions plant in Tulsa failed, and he was unable to get a synthetic rubber factory agreement.

Eventually Rhodes discovered that the major deterrent to his efforts was Tulsa's lack of adequate housing for incoming families. The shortage was especially acute for small furnished low-income apartments and three-room frame houses. The Roosevelt administration had estimated that before any major project could locate in Tulsa the city would need to construct 4,000 to 5,000 new residences within an intermediate price range. National functionaries announced their willingness to construct half of those needed if local construction firms would build the remainder. City leaders reasoned that after the war, if workers should leave the community, black residents could occupy the homes and thus help solve the chronic overcrowding in the Greenwood neighborhood. Although the overseas struggle drained Tulsa construction-material stockpiles, making shortages at home, the chamber managed to underwrite several housing projects; furthermore the city council temporarily waived a number of the building code regulations that were important to insure quality but might have slowed progress. Near the end of 1942 the Federal Housing Administration had constructed what became known as "war apartments," consisting of two-story, dormitory-like dwellings. Single persons lived in one- or two-room apartments and married couples lived in those a bit larger. Although the new buildings somewhat alleviated the demand, their number fell far short of what Tulsa needed, and the occupancy problem remained throughout the war and the ensuing fifteen years.

Other Midwestern and Southwestern cities besides Tulsa coveted the federal money poured into East- and West-Coast metropolises. Understanding that numbers often meant strength, Tulsa, Kansas City, Fort Worth, Omaha, and Dallas joined together in a Midwest Defense Conference (MDC) and sent spokespersons to the nation's capital. For its MDC cooperation, Tulsa reaped handsome dividends when an influence peddler wired then chamber president Victor Barnett that the War Department would build a Tulsa branch plant for Consolidated Aircraft Corporation. Chamber members reacted to the news with wide grins and backslapping. An airplane factory meant $11 million in public construction, a total exceeding any previous yearly volume in city history.

The cheers quickly turned to frowns when, within two weeks,

President Barnett informed co-workers that the Fort Worth Chamber of Commerce was fighting the decision and bringing Consolidated to Texas. John Dunkin jumped to his feet and furiously exclaimed, "Oklahoma has lost every cockeyed project so far!" The directors quickly organized a special committee of Rhodes, Waite Phillips, Otis McClintock, Victor F. Barnett, L. W. Grant, Sam Clammer, John Rogers, Elmo Thompson, and John D. Mayo, who immediately went to Washington, D.C. and conferred with War Department decision makers, while William G. Skelly flew to San Diego to meet with executives of Consolidated Aircraft Corporation. On Capitol Hill the Tulsans met with Oklahoma Congressman Wesley Disney who soothed them by saying, "Don't be alarmed over anything that may appear to be bad news." The travelers received additional assurances that same day from War Department authority Colonel William H. Harrison who telephoned President Barnett and ordered, "Sit tight and don't lose your nerve."

Reassured, Rhodes flew from Washington to San Diego to help Skelly. On December 15, 1940 the two men met with James Fleet, president of Consolidated, and Rhodes informed him of the last few days' conversations. Skelly asked Fleet why he objected to Tulsa, and the president replied that Consolidated specialized in seaplanes and that, unlike Tulsa, Fort Worth had a lake suitable for operating. The two Tulsans returned home the following day, concerned with Fleet's recalcitrant attitude but convinced that the federal people would hold to their pledge. On December 25, 1940 the War Department announced that Tulsa had been designated the site for an aircraft assembly plant; but Consolidated had also won a victory. On January 7, 1941 a War Department spokesperson announced that the Douglas Aircraft Company, not Consolidated, had agreed to station itself in Tulsa. In any case, chamber tenacity had won the day, and after the Douglas plant opened its assembly line, the Spartan School of Aeronautics began training American and British pilots; moreover, Tulsa became a center for the aircraft industry for more than two decades.

The 1942 Tulsa Armistice Day celebration, commemorating the anniversary of the first Great War's end, occurred after the United States had officially entered the war. The city event therefore gave persons a chance to display their invigorated patriotism and newfound economic strength. Opening the festivities, a rider on horseback carrying a large American flag led floats of all shapes and sizes that paraded before a crowd of 10,000 men, women, and children. That afternoon and evening farmers, bankers, housewives, high-school students, and World War I veterans crowded into the fair-grounds and approvingly inspected military displays of rifles, uniforms, and artillery.

Affirming the will to win took other forms. Residents staged annual aluminum drives for the troops overseas; the first, on July 6, 1941, netted more than 40,000 pounds. The major civic activity was, however, the inevitable war-bond campaign, necessary for financing the cause. In the first drive Lenard M. Grant, chairman of the Tulsa County War-Bond Campaign, sent pledge cards to public and private schools, and teachers distributed them among students who then took them home to their parents. The family that signed received a decal for proud display on its front door. After the push ended, Grant paid high-school students to go door to door soliciting from those with no sticker, who already suffered a social stigma. Grant led six drives during the war, and the most successful was in May of 1942 when his team collected pledges totaling $7,864,024; however, the 1944 campaign netted $1 million in one day. The generosity was even more impressive considering the fact that inflated wartime prices for necessities devalued most peoples' incomes.

American soldiers on active duty in Europe and Asia needed sugar, rubber, coffee, fruit, vegetables, and gasoline, and those who remained at home sacrificed. The federal government, as it had done during the Depression, instituted a food-stamp rationing program for consumer goods, and most Tulsans gladly participated. The seals came in a series, and each bearer exchanged his or hers for a designated item and quantity. Customers purchased fruits and vegetables in five-pound crates or received gasoline in exchange for the coupons. Tulsans used saccharin as a substitute for sugar and nylon in place of rubber, and every homemaker saved old grease in the skillet for the next meal. The system placed a hardship on the average person, but repayment came with the feeling that one was contributing to a democratic cause. Tulsans savored such an attitude, which made the division they experienced in the twenties and the despair they lived with in the thirties seem far away.

Although a degree of prosperity and confidence was returning, futurists feared that without the war their city's financial health might return to late 1930s recession conditions. Chamber general manager Rhodes reported to his colleagues that non-defense-oriented concerns found labor in short supply, because workers earned higher pay in war industries; yet "the [fighting] will not last forever," Rhodes said, and Tulsa must "start now to fortify against the letdown." The Post-Emergency Planning Board was the city's agency responsible for preventing a slowdown. Mayor Veale, his staff, and chamber organizers founded it two weeks before the bombing of Pearl Harbor and ordered the participants to determine how to "lessen the impact of . . . change." Chairman Clyde King divided researchers into two groups: one to investigate current productivity and manpower within the Tulsa industrial area, and the second to draw up chamber and city council recommendations on how Tulsa should prepare for the end of a wartime productivity. The first sub-committee submitted a questionnaire to major firms asking about their plans for employing returning veterans, for implementing worker training programs, and for offering new jobs for present defense-plant personnel. The King staff assessment was optimistic, asserting that 86 percent of Tulsa-manufactured items were not necessarily connected with war, and thus their marketability should remain constant. The committee predicted that agricultural prices would even rise, and survey results indicated that citizens had a positive outlook. More than 7,000 families expected to buy automobiles after the war, promising estimated sales for local car dealers as high as $6,309,900; and 2,938 persons planned to build new homes within two years, assuring the construction industry that it could reasonably expect a gross income of approximately $13,645,000, King's team contended. Concurring, Charles C. Clark, director of the War Housing Center, a bureau of the city government, noted that a need for houses would rise after 1945, because 75 percent of the mid-forties demand had come from people not involved in war related jobs.

There was, as city officials knew, a darker side to the bright predictions, for an increasing request for consumer goods meant inflation. As early as mid-summer of 1946 retail stores reported heavy buying; grocers predicted that the price of meat would accelerate thirteen to twenty cents per pound after the war, and residential rent was rising at a rate varying between 25 and 100 percent. Real estate owners lamented that repair costs had doubled from 1941 to 1946 and that their lease charge increases therefore were justified.

United States government alleviated the problem as it had done in 1942. The Federal Housing Administration promised to build 100 units at federal expense, sell them at $7,500 each, and construct an additional 60 for rental. Local builders, not wanting to be left out of the profits, reported to the Public Service Corporation, in November of 1946, that if federal money should continue, contractors could build ten homes a day. That particular piece of news fell on welcome ears, for by June of 1951 the *Daily Oklahoman* reported that Tulsa still had a massive residence shortage.

The chamber pleaded with President Harry S. Truman to lift wartime price controls on commodities, in the belief that supply needed to catch up with demand. The president's advisors argued the same line, and Truman eventually abolished the restrictions; however, the results were shattering, for Tulsans immediately felt the effects of the worst inflationary spiral of the twentieth century. Coffee prices doubled from five to ten cents per pound, and other retail sales climbed 22 percent during the first nine months of 1946. Exorbitant prices were bad for consumers as well as sellers but had one good effect on blue-collar workers. Beginning in January of 1945 Tulsa businesses found themselves short of manpower, which drove hourly wages up to $1.19. Entrepreneurs blamed the federal government's salary controls and war-production inducements which, the Tulsans claimed, handicapped firms dealing in peacetime commodities. City government officeholders countered that, eventually, returning servicemen would bring an end to high payrolls, a prediction that proved incorrect, for by the decade's end annual family income in Tulsa reached $4,530, a figure much greater than the national average.

Labor costs and an insufficient water supply frightened away several prospective firms after 1945. The city council therefore looked for a new reservoir when, in 1946, local consumption rose from 25 million to 30 million gallons. City water department researchers estimated that Tulsa had to have 40 percent more water by the end of the decade if current levels were maintained. They recommended to Mayor Olney Flynn that engineers add six feet to

Mohawk Dam, increasing the lake's storage capacity by 8 million gallons. Soon the people sanctioned $3 million in bonds, by a 9,146 to 1,311 vote margin, for extending and remodeling the dams at Spavinaw and Mohawk lakes and the water mains leading into the city. The by-product was that old and new companies began expanding. For instance, by 1949 Mid-Continent Petroleum finished a 45,000-barrel-capacity plant, and the Texas Company, from Galveston, established a new 21,000-barrel refinery in West Tulsa south of the Arkansas River.

The quickened growth extended throughout the next ten years. Significantly, Webster High School students helped the city commemorate forty-five years of advancement by presenting and installing a plaque on Highway 66 near the site of old Number One at Red Fork. Tulsans purchased new and used automobiles at a record rate; contractors erected downtown offices so rapidly that the total value equaled one-fifth of all state construction. In 1956 Gulf Oil acquired William K. Warren's petroleum company and occupied the modern Gulf-Western Building on South Boulder. Before the end of World War II Tulsa added Braniff Airways and American Airlines to the number of companies providing service to major cities in the United States, Latin America, and Europe. Local air transport firms also prospered, and in January of 1945 Mid-Continent Airlines received a federally approved contract from New Orleans for a nonstop flight between the oil capital and the Mardi Gras center. Tulsans paid a series of taxes from 1945 to 1960 totaling $350,000 for an auxiliary airport and $4,200,000 for a terminal building at Tulsa Municipal, which replaced the original structure built in 1928.

The predominantly conservative Tulsa attitude was that company profits were good not only for owners, but also for public servants and the people whom firms employed, and the belief brought hordes of new migrants. By 1960 the city's inhabitants numbered 261,685, a figure that had more than doubled since the Depression's onset, and most of the growth had occurred after 1940. Forty shopping centers developed between 1945 and 1950, a phenomenon unmatched in the United States by any other city of comparable size. Chamber activities and accomplishments became even more numerous than during the oil boom days, so the organization moved its offices into a private Boston Avenue building on March 21, 1952.

During the 1940s and 1950s, commercial interests and citizens' groups alike used the city's forty-three public schools to support "Americanism" and promodernization stances. As formerly mentioned, students purchased War Savings Stamps and Bonds and conducted several scrap-paper and -metal drives. In addition they "adopted" servicemen, to whom they wrote letters and sent cookies. The federal government doled out funds for public-education-centered child care, catering to defense-plant workers' children, and from 1941 to 1943 the system also provided training facilities for 30,000 soldiers.

Despite their many contributions, in June of 1942 Richard Lloyd Jones reported to the chamber that teachers' salaries had not risen from a base pay of $1,530 since the height of the Depression, in 1935, although Department of Labor statistics indicated that the cost of living had increased by 20 percent. Gradual increases began during the late forties; by 1947, women holding bachelors' degrees made $1,900, and similarly-qualified men earned $2,200, only $300 more per year than they had commanded in 1928. The Tulsa school board finally raised the base pay, in 1948, to $2,400 and $2,200 for men and women, respectively. A master's degree entitled an educator to an additional $200 annually, and after four years' experience one could receive an additional $300 annually. Senior and junior high principals made $5,400, and those leading elementary schools received $5,200. During the mid-fifties men took $3,154 and women, $2,970 as base pay, while principals edged up to between $4,770 and $6,450. In 1957, ten years after Mrs. William Guier, the second female board president, took office, the starting remunerations for women were at last commensurate with those for men; by 1960, however, amounts for both sexes still fell below national averages.

A significant number of educators earned extra pay by teaching in night school, an innovative idea that the board first conceived, in 1949, for student "improvement, advancement, recreation, and enjoyment, in addition to helping adults earn graduation certificates." Evening classes brought new pupils and made the steps toward earning a diploma easier for adults. On the practical side, the augmented curriculum also gave administrators a reason to lobby for more state appropriations. In 1950 the system had 36,777 matriculants, and by 1960 it listed 65,638, although many were returning pupils. To accommodate them all, between 1948 and 1959 the city built forty new schools. Another educational promotion was a summer conference held once every two years at the University of Tulsa from the mid-1940s to the early 1960s. Each session consisted of a two-week seminar featuring nationally known experts, and as many as 1,000 teachers participated in one peak year. Although some progressive changes occurred, the right-wing political and economic mood of the nation mirrored itself in the Tulsa school system. Even before World War II in December of 1940, the board made a public statement promising to inculcate "democratic" values within pupils and to ferret out any liberal teachers or textbooks. Subsequently, throughout the next twenty years, city officials and residents conducted periodic "witch hunts," and frequently the board expelled "students who refused to participate in patriotic ceremonies" that the state superintendent of public instruction prescribed; moreover, during many of these years at Tulsa area schools the chamber conducted Education-Business Day which applauded the merits of "trickle-down" economic theory.

Tulsa education also held fast to segregation for the approximately 5,500 black students who attended separate schools. The board also waited five years after the 1954 *Brown vs. Topeka Board of Education* United States Supreme Court case declaring such institutions unconstitutional before making any moves to eliminate them. In 1959 Tulsans redrew districts, creating a few integrated buildings. The board concurrently asserted that any parent could request that his or her child attend classrooms in which his or her race was in the majority, sapping what little strength was in the original measure. During the next few years an increasingly mobile black population did reach out of Greenwood and occupy other areas of the city, and its children attended formerly all-white schools such as Burroughs, Emerson, and Roosevelt. White flight away from black encroachment, however, soon left new neighborhoods segregated as well.

The majority of black citizens remained impoverished, as they had been for forty years. Chauncey Border, chairman of a temporary chamber task force, noted in a treatise that the city must produce a program for improving black neighborhoods. Border urged the Tulsa government to convince Federal Housing Administration bureaucrats to erect dwellings and rent them for fifteen dollars a month; he further insisted that city housing inspectors condemn dilapidated homes and edifices and that Health Department workers enforce sanitary requirements already on the statute books. The well researched and documented Border statements painted such a dismal picture of the living conditions that a number of responsible city and business officials proposed, to no avail, that the old Greenwood section be completely abandoned and its dwellers relocated. Building new structures, however, would not alter the institutional racism that infected Tulsa. The black unemployment rate stood at more than 11 percent, a figure higher than that within the white community, although not much worse than in the late twenties. The vast majority of blacks did not have skills and therefore faced being the last persons hired for a job and the first ones fired. War industries hired minorities, and a few firms such as Douglas Aircraft employed them in skilled positions, but many company policies held that black people performed best in jobs requiring no special skill. Even the city government employed only 77 blacks among 864 city workers. Only one held an executive position, seventeen worked for the police department, and the remainder served as street sweepers and garbage collectors.

Some of the blame for the poor economic conditions fell on minorities themselves. Investigators from the National Urban League found more diversity of black-owned business in Tulsa than in any other United States city of comparable size. Standard establishments included barber shops, grocery stores, cafes, cleaners, mortuaries, real estate agencies, furniture stores, and building contractors. Urban League investigators concluded that black shopkeepers discriminated against and distrusted their brothers and sisters, preferring to think of themselves as better than the masses of "shiftless niggers." Such diversity, the Urban League assessed, was a retarding factor in racial improvement.

The Creeks' century-old problem was thus echoed among Tulsa's most recent class of rejected persons; however, for several reasons, negro handicaps toward assimilation were even greater than the Indians' had been. First of all, the old Indian Territorial missionaries had a significant impact on the white socialization of many Creeks, and oftentimes the financial remunerations for whites who married Indians during the nineteenth and early twentieth centuries were great. Many whites and their offspring benefitted materially from Indian spouses' land and oil rights. Black people therefore suffered prejudice from both Indians and whites, whose ancestors had owned slaves and rooted their materialistic interests in Tulsa. Finally, the marked skin color difference between blacks and other racial groups always earmarked the former as somehow different from other human beings. The segregated therefore remained blighted. Fewer than one-third of their homes had indoor toilets, and only one-fourth included indoor baths. The majority of black families subsisted in a communal-apartment-house existence, with one bathroom to a floor; often more than one shared a two-room place. For this "luxurious" accommodation each household head paid sixteen to twenty-five dollars a month rent. Poverty bred crime. Although blacks composed 10 percent of the population, they committed 33 percent of all crimes, of which they, themselves, were frequently the victims. The most common offenses were loitering, public drunkenness, and carrying a concealed weapon.

While minority Tulsans languished, civic leaders concentrated their efforts on educational and artistic endeavors. Tulsa University (TU) also reflected conservative principles and opened a college of law specializing in real estate and petroleum law. In 1957 administrators noted the fiftieth anniversary of the school with a fund drive for $5 million to pay for eleven new school buildings over the next ten years. The endeavor was successful. Overseers built and dignitaries dedicated Lottie Jane, John Mabee, and Phillips halls, added to the Wesley Center. Simultaneous to TU improvements, in 1965 an Oklahoma protestant faith healer opened another private college, naming it after himself, Oral Roberts University. Twelve years later the Oral Roberts Association moved the school to its present location in southern Tulsa; there it became a religious and education center for young Christian men and women throughout the world, as well as an architectural extravaganza.

While the money spent on education soared, culture followed close behind. In 1939 the Waite Phillips family donated its mansion to the city as a museum. Surrounded by twenty-three acres of land, the Philbrook Art Center quickly became a mecca for connoisseurs and tourists from all over the Southwest and the rest of the nation. Three years later Thomas Gilcrease, a Creek oilman, banker, and world traveler, established a depository for books and historical artifacts, primarily to preserve the American Indian heritage. Although whites had wrested Tulsa from Creek control, Gilcrease acknowledged his race's debt by selling his collection to the city in 1955 for a total of $2,250,000, an extremely low price. During the first years of city ownership, wealthy Tulsans freely spent their money to preserve and augment the Gilcrease Museum. In their drive to create the cultural center of Oklahoma, wealthy and concerned citizens paid for erection of the Tulsa Civic Center, which housed city and county offices, a new library, and the symphony headquarters. In addition traveling ballet companies and entertainers performed in the auditorium before enthusiastic audiences. By the mid-sixties, Tulsans had made their city the aesthetic nexus of the state and of high rank in the Southwest.

Although the Tulsa elite gave money and time to enrich the city's personality, their politics, like those of many middle-class natives, were fiscally conservative. The war ended deflation, and late forties inflation seemed to castigate Democratic Keynesian spending. Tulsans now felt free again to espouse and embrace their frontier individualism. The local election results of 1940 illustrated a fear that President Roosevelt was ending the two-party system. That year the Republicans nominated Olney F. Flynn, a longtime resident and owner of the Flynn Oil Company, to challenge Mayor Veale's attempt for a third consecutive term. Veale misjudged deeply rooted attitudes and followed his usual political tactic of mouthing New Deal wonders. Unfortunately for him, Flynn defeated Veale by 5,000 votes and led a Republican sweep of all city offices. It looked as though Veale might stave off the impending GOP ascendancy when he returned, in 1942, to run against Republican businessman Charles R. Niven. Roosevelt's popularity in Tulsa had made a sudden recovery after the Japanese bombed Pearl Harbor, and Democrats like Veale willingly pledged their full allegiance to country, God, Tulsa, and the President, in that order. Although Veale triumphed that year, Flynn returned victorious in 1944, but left his city position after a term to run for governor of Oklahoma against Democrat cattleman Roy Turner. Flynn lost, but he threw his local support in the Tulsa mayoral contest to Lee Price, also an affluent Republican, who faced Patrick Mallory, a local attorney and World War II veteran. Although the Democratic challenger attracted thousands of supporters because of his years of overseas fighting, his heroism was not enough, and in a heavy turnout the people chose Price and the entire GOP slate.

The nationwide election of 1948 was by all standards one of the most unusual and exciting in American history, and Tulsans had a similar experience of their own. Thomas Dewey, the Republican presidential contender, trounced President Harry S Truman in Tulsa, just as the statisticians had predicted; yet the city Republican Party found itself bitterly divided over the so-called "Cochrane Plan" to build a super-expressway around the city at a taxpayer cost of $6,650,000. Mayor Price defeated his primary opposition and in the general race faced Roy Lundy, a Tulsa investor since 1910. Lundy opposed the Cochrane program and questioned the wisdom of purchasing for destruction fifty homes on future super-highway land. Conversely, Price gave his solid support to the proposition and proclaimed, "I will go up or . . . down on this expressway [issue]."

Other Republicans were not so willing to make the same judgment. Republican finance commissioner John M. Hall, considered by experts to have the best chance of reelection, neither publicly opposed nor supported the mayor, preferring to keep his own counsel on the matter. Joseph R. McGraw, the GOP nominee for city police chief, openly split with Price over the issue, and feelings became so heated between the two men that the mayor's strategists ordered McGraw out of a tactics session and threatened to withdraw support from his campaign.

Lundy and the other Democrats gleefully exposed the divided opposition, asserting that the new highway would mean higher taxes and that the Republican administration was deliberately not spending $2,100 in road bonds from a 1945 referendum in an attempt to make the street problem most serious. When the political dust cleared, Tulsans marched to the polls in record numbers and cast 33,707 votes. Winning, Lundy received 17,755 of them, and most of the other Democrats also grasped victories.

President Truman's economic policies and United Nations (U.N.) intervention in Korea dominated the Tulsa and national political scene for the next five years. Locals paid heavily in inflated prices and wages, and every time each rose, some facet of the city hated the chief executive more. They nonetheless willingly fought North Korean aggression. The president called on the Tulsa Marine Corps Reserve unit of 262 men and officers and Company B, Twentieth Infantry, composed of men from the northeastern corner of Oklahoma, to leave for South Korea on August 1, 1950. Once again Tulsans wrestled to squelch or contain the enemies of democracy.

The "police action" went badly at first for U.N. troops, composed mostly of Americans, but when the tide slowly turned, U.N. Commander and former World War II star General Douglas MacArthur once again became a national hero. An open polemic between President Truman and MacArthur over the question of bombing Communist Chinese airfields and cities blossomed to such an extent that the commander-in-chief dismissed his underling. Although generals George C. Marshall (then Secretary of State) and Omar Bradley agreed with the President, many Americans cried out in protest.

Fear of communism, which Senator Joseph McCarthy's antics whetted, tempered the nation's mood. Tulsans followed suit and denounced the President and his action. Letters from citizens in support and sympathy for the dethroned military man flooded the editors' desks at the two major Tulsa newspapers. The polity's disbelief quickly turned into vitriolic attacks against President Truman. Richard Lloyd Jones wrote, "Every true American citizen should rise up in outrage and in indignation to demand that Truman be impeached." The next day Republicans, smelling political blood, held a public meeting and passed a resolution calling for the president's removal. The movement died almost as quickly as it had begun, but in the national elections of 1952 Tulsans registered discontent and voted two to one for Republican presidential aspirant Dwight D. Eisenhower.

Neither 1950, 1952, nor 1954 was a good year for FDR's once triumphant party. Harley Van Cleave, an oil executive and political novice, surprisingly upset Mayor Lundy in the primary but then lost the general election of 1950 to Republican George Stoner, the popular three-term street commissioner. History repeated itself in the next city race but reversed sides for the primary. Republican Charles M. Warren, a former municipal judge, pitted himself against Van Cleave who ran on a Democratic platform that was oriented toward industrial blue-collar workers all the time. The party received heavy support from the local American Federation of Labor and the Congress of Industrial Organizations. Families volunteered their children for door-to-door canvassing and organized rallies for the party. The general election had few fireworks but brought Tulsans to the polls in record numbers, and they voted heavily for the entire Republican ticket. The GOP candidates made victory look easy in 1954 when L. C. Clark, a retired hardware dealer, defeated John W. McCune, an attorney, in an election distinctive from the preceding one only because Elizabeth Stowell Anderson became the first woman since 1920 to win the position of city auditor.

In the election of 1956, a hot contest, Mayor Clark opposed George E. Norvell, a county judge. Two issues overshadowed all others–the need for higher city taxes and retention of a civil service system for city employees. This time both candidates catered to conservatism and opposed the assessment issue, but Norvell supported retention of the latter and carried the Democrats to victory by 10,000 votes. It was their first since 1948, overcoming an Eisenhower landslide that buried presidential aspirant Stevenson for the second time in four years.

If the Democrats looked forward to a "honeymoon period" in city government, they were quickly disappointed when city commissioners Jay Jones, Patrick McGuire, and Fay Young immediately voted to submit a referendum to repeal Tulsa service employment practices. Angered, Norvell vetoed the action and bitterly denounced it as an attempt to destroy professionalization of "a body of well trained, alert public servants. . . ." The League of Women Voters, a non-partisan organization of politically active women, quickly came to the mayor's side. In a letter to the city council, President Alma Elder equated government with business and stressed that the merit system provided "superior organization." The Tulsa Business and Professional Women's Club, Incorporated, joined the forces, decrying, ". . . our organization felt it important for progressive and well operated government. . . ." Within a week the discussion degenerated into personal attack. H. A. Norberg, chairman of the Civil Service Board, accused Police Commissioner Jones of using the spoils system in his appointment of two policemen while passing over thirteen persons who had better scores on qualifying examinations. Commissioner Jones retorted that he was a misunderstood man. "What we must have," he argued, "and what I want is an amendment to the city charter." By this time tempers had begun to cool, and Mayor Norvell agreed to place a referendum before the people to make a merit system part of the Tulsa Charter, and the body politic overwhelmingly approved.

The affair brought statewide notoriety to Tulsa and to Norvell, prompting him to run for lieutenant governor of the state in 1958. The door thus opened for more neophytes when flower shop owner James L. Maxwell beat John McCune in the Democratic Party primary and then battled for the key spot with Jack Hadley, vice-president of the Midwestern Instrument Company. The contest began and ended on a friendly note, and each man conducted a clean bid, devoid of backbiting. The major issue was the changing of the structure of city government to reflect more centralized power, a stance that both candidates supported. Maxwell and the Democrats won the day, making him at thirty-one years of age the youngest person ever elected Tulsa's mayor; and in 1958 the people recalled him for another term.

The Maxwell election symbolized the end of an era and the beginning of a new one for Tulsans. They had in one century established commercial ties by highway, railroad, and airway with every major city in the United States and foreign countries in Latin America, Western Europe, and East Asia. Politicos were already discussing the possibility of joining their city to the world by water. In 1945 Tulsa had been faced, as had the entire nation, with the decision of whether or not to continue the New Deal's "half-century of revolution," as historian Eric Goldman has called it. Goldman contended that the nation's federal representatives, under a liberal Truman and a moderate Eisenhower, had persevered and decided by 1960 to commit the country to another decade of social reform. Although Tulsa had *temporarily* closed the door on many federally bolstered, collective concepts except those that aided industrial development, it still held fast to city government reform and cultural and educational embellishment projects.

VIII

The Modern City

Tulsans experienced spectacular commercial development during the 1960s and 1970s, while the multitudes of people who swelled the inhabitants' ranks also demanded city services and social change. As early as 1965 one-fourth of the nation's residents lived within 500 miles of Tulsa—an area stretching from New Orleans, Louisiana; north to St. Louis, Missouri; west to Denver, Colorado; and south to Houston, Texas. The most striking characteristic of the population and economic surge, which only oil-boom days had paralleled, was that it forced Tulsans to diversify their business interests. Although 21,081 people worked for oil companies in 1965, within the next fifteen years several organizations had moved their headquarters to Houston; but Tulsa suffered no dramatic damage. Midway through the decade of the sixties, the city claimed 812 diversified manufacturers, which employed 30,000 people with an annual payroll in excess of $153 million. There were 40 companies working 100 men and women each, 26 with at least 200, and 5 with more than 1,000. Business-district modernization costs during only one year, 1965, reached $67 million, for the city, like other sun-belt regions, was attracting new firms at a record rate. Office space quadrupled so as to shelter new businesses like Rockwell International, which established a branch in April of 1962 within a city block of the Tulsa International Airport. Rockwell manufactured the structures for the world's largest passenger jets and components for the Apollo and Saturn rockets. In addition, that same year North American Aviation leased a section of the Douglas plant complex from the United States Air Force.

Although Tulsa was weaning itself from the petroleum industry, the city's fortunes, like those of the rest of the nation, were inextricably tied, throughout the sixties and early seventies, to the supplies needed to remain involved in the Vietnam conflict, resulting in President John Kennedy's, and then primarily President Lyndon Johnson's, "guns-and-butter" policy. As a result, the local economy inflated and then, during the mid-1970s, entered a recession of shorter duration and milder intensity than in other metropolitan centers around the country. By 1975 national forecasters predicted a recovery, but conditions volleyed back and forth throughout the decade.

One major reason that Tulsa weathered the earlier withdrawal of major oil headquarters and uncertain economic times was the completion of the Arkansas River Navigation System and the opening of the Port of Catoosa, in June of 1971. The dedication ceremonies, at which President Richard M. Nixon was present, ended more than half a century of planning and fulfilled the dream of United States senators John McClellan, of Arkansas, and Robert S. Kerr. The crusade for an inland waterway up the Arkansas River began in 1909 when Assistant United States Engineer William Parkin surveyed the river and found that seafaring was feasible. He proposed construction of four locks, at Tulsa, Muskogee, Fort Smith, and Little Rock, all at a cost he estimated at $2 million, much of which the federal government would pay.

Interest spread within the minds of northeastern Oklahoma traders. In December of 1911, two years after Parkin publicly announced his findings, the chamber of commerce sent a delegate to the National Rivers and Harbors Congress, composed of Department of the Interior personnel and private citizen representatives, all concerned about the effect of trafficking on major North American rivers. Two weeks after the convention, Tulsans discovered an unexpected champion, Champ Clark, speaker of the United States House of Representatives and leading contender for the Democratic presidential nomination. He won the hearts of an overflow public gathering by pledging his support for renovating the thoroughfare.

Citizens of small rural communities also joined the quest for a federal project, especially after the river overflowed its banks three times in five years after World War I. Army engineers seconded the Oklahomans, but not until the great Mississippi River flood in 1927, which took the lives of fifteen people and caused several million dollars' worth of property damage, did Congress and President Calvin Coolidge sign into law the River and Harbor Act of 1927 authorizing a preliminary examination and survey of the Arkansas and Red rivers.

In July of that year 350 delegates including congressmen, officials of the War and Agriculture departments, and independently motivated persons from a dozen states, conferred in Tulsa. They organized the Arkansas River Flood Control Association and elected Clarence B. Douglas as president. In 1929 the original organization had evolved into the Arkansas River Association, made Little Rock, Arkansas the home base, and commissioned Douglas to take up permanent residence in Washington. That year, also, Tulsa joined the Mississippi Valley Association which comprised virtually the same membership as did the Arkansas River Association, expanding its influence into the deep South. The former contracted with engineer Theodore Bent, of New Orleans, for a study of transportation possibilities and their estimated costs. Bent aired his findings in January of 1931 at a St. Louis conference, during which he estimated that water transportation was tied directly to Tulsa's fiscal tomorrows. Houston was rapidly becoming a major seaport, and there was growing concern that the Texas community would soon outstrip all other Southwestern industrial centers.

The last United States Congress before World War II fighting began stressed the need for a comprehensive flood control plan, but Pearl Harbor halted further investigations. While American soldiers battled, however, the waterway movement found a charismatic leader, Robert S. Kerr. As governor of Oklahoma from 1943 to 1947, he dedicated his efforts to ending the disastrous overflows that plagued farmers and shopkeepers in northeastern Oklahoma and to developing a cheap, competitive transport service at the same time. As state chief executive, Kerr authorized an Oklahoma study that described the great advantages of opening the river to intercourse. Kerr's people prophesied that annually the waterway would carry 419,000 tons of wheat at a consumer savings of $1,270,000. They also predicted that more than 50 percent of the oil produced in the Southwest would travel via the river and that the per-ton cost to ship gas from Tulsa to Little Rock would drop from the $5.20 railroad fee to $.99. After his gubernatorial term Kerr went on to serve as a United States senator, his promise unfulfilled; thus by the end of World War II the desire became an obsession with many Tulsans. "This town," said Glade Kirkpatrick, chairman of the chamber Waterways Committee, "cannot live and continue to grow without this [Arkansas River] development."

Tulsa's persistent pleas began exerting additional political pressure on Congress through the Mississippi Valley Association, and finally, on July 24, 1946, at an expense of $1.2 billion, the nation's lawmakers authorized excavation on the Arkansas River and its tributaries to facilitate travel, assure flood control, and generate hydroelectric power. Senator Kerr won a seat on the Senate Rivers and Harbors Subcommittee and guided the project to its completion. Through political barter he successfully surmounted potential roadblocks during the Kennedy administration, assisting the young president with other legislative programs in return for Kennedy's support of the navigation plan. After Kerr's untimely death on New Year's Day in 1963, United States Senator Mike Monroney and Congressman Carl Albert, both from Oklahoma, carried on the fight, and when, in January of 1964, President Lyndon Johnson proposed an $84 million cut in the program's budget they convinced him to change his mind.

Signifying the project's completion, on December 30, 1970 the Corps of Engineers' workboats *Sallisaw* and *Arkoma* sailed up the waterway. The first incoming cargo ship to the Port of Catoosa arrived on January 21, 1971 bearing newsprint for the *World* and the *Tribune*. Soon Oklahoma Panhandle wheat, Texas beef, and Southwestern petroleum flowed down the river. Tulsans were now linked to the international community because sailors could transport goods directly to a United States coastal port and on to a foreign country; moreover, during the late 1970s officials established a foreign trade zone at the waterway center.

An international thoroughfare was not enough for the ambitious. The Tulsa World Trade Association consistently lobbied to bring

Tulsa's Gilcrease Museum. (*Courtesy of the Beryl Ford Collection, Tulsa, Oklahoma*)

This view of Tulsa was taken from the entrance of Chandler Park, which is approximately three and one-half miles west of downtown Tulsa. This is Twenty-first Street in foreground. (*Courtesy of Mr. Eddie DuPree, Stillwater, Oklahoma*)

to the city overseas companies. It has been successful, for the European Hilti AG, the K. M. Kinshofer Corporation of West Germany, and International American Ceramics all have headquarters in the city. As a result, the airport now contains United States Customs and Department of Commerce Port of Origin offices.

Beginning with the Catoosa Port opening, worldwide trade swelled the ranks of financially satisfied Tulsans. Annual family incomes exceeded the national average, while only 16 percent of the population earned less than $3,000 a year, compared to 19 percent nationwide. Forty-three cents out of every dollar went for food and housing, and Tulsans spent twelve cents per hundred for transportation. Retail sales during the sixties climbed rapidly as many folk achieved an ever-expanding standard of living. The year 1963 saw automobile sales jump 21 percent, food 20 percent, and retail store merchandise 15 percent above the previous year; thus Johnson's Great Society years witnessed surging affluence for many Americans, especially Tulsans.

Statistics on housing, however, were misleading. The historic problem of an inadequate supply continued. Under the Housing Act of 1961 the federal government granted $136,275 to Tulsa for building low-cost homes, after city investigators revealed what everyone already knew–that the lower the family income in Tulsa, the higher percentage of the resource went to pay for shelter. Those making less than $3,000 annually spent one-third of their incomes for monthly rents or house payments, while individuals earning $10,000 and more spent 10 percent or less. Such figures indicated a widening gap between economic classes, a condition that the city knew it must abate.

The civil rights movement and the impact of Johnson's poverty programs put pressure on local governments to improve the quality of living for Tulsa's less fortunate. Under the direction of the city council and the Demonstration Agency, local experts investigated social, economic, and political conditions of the indigent and made suggestions to alleviate the despicable environments within which almost one-fourth of the city's population lived. Change agents, striving to close the economic gap between the lower- and middle-income groups, pinpointed a need for improved educational opportunities, especially those related to job training. The median education level for black households was eleven and two-tenths years, compared to twelve and three-tenths for the total population. Other unpleasant statistics were that the black family breadwinners never received occupational training; thus they filled menial positions, which paid less than skilled jobs. The National Urban League's Tulsa outpost attempted to deal with the problem by arranging career apprenticeships, but the organization lacked sufficient funding and numbers of firms willing to participate. Because self-help schemes failed to break down barriers throughout the nation, the Civil Rights acts of 1964 and 1965 targeted for destruction discrimination in Tulsa and other cities. Serious problems remain, however, a fact that farsighted persons continue to point out. In public addresses, Joseph Williams, president of the Williams Company, has emphasized the crying need for economic revival among poor blacks living primarily in the city's north side. Ironically Tulsa faces shortages of skilled laborers in fields such as metal working, while some languish in poverty. Says Williams:

> Racism is still the number one problem in Tulsa. . . . It has distorted our growth patterns and in fact is the real reason that the goal of balanced growth for our community is not being realized.

Public education has also made slow but measured strides toward providing equal educational opportunities. Almost fifteen years after *Brown vs. Board of Education* decried segregation, the school board redrew districts to create a semblance of integration in the public school system. The overseers also altered the transfer policy permitting any student movement to a school in which his race was in a majority. In 1968 the supervisors relocated 184 instructors in an attempt to racially intermingle staffs. The action disgorged volcanic teacher, student, and parent protest, especially from whites. The Tulsa superintendent slowed the procedures, and by 1970 a federal court declared him recalcitrant, forcing administrators to move more educators so that the white–black faculty ratio in each school was around eighty-eight to twelve, respectively. The figure has remained relatively true to current classroom realities.

In further compliance with court determinations against Tulsa, the school board formulated and submitted an unacceptable blueprint for junior- and senior-high integration to the United States Department of Justice in March of 1971. In July national and state forces compromised, and a strategy went into action for the

1971–72 year. The board authorized construction of four new schools: Mason and Washington senior, and Thoreau and Foster junior, highs. Rezoning and busing to shuffle student bodies were also part of the proposal; however, five middle schools went unfettered, and the board closed Carver Junior High.

The decision to lock up, rather than renovate, the formerly all-black Carver added to the anger of Tulsa liberals and a majority of blacks because this action meant that more blacks than whites would have to motor far from home to obtain an education. To still hostility the board invited citizens to a public meeting in which

From atop the Williams Center Tower, looking directly south. The tallest building in the picture is the First Bank of Oklahoma; the tall white building to the right is the Cities Service Building; and the dark glass-front building in front of Cities Service is the Fourth National Bank. Construction to the bottom right of the Cities Service Building is to be tied to both buildings. (*Courtesy of Mr. Eddie DuPree, Stillwater, Oklahoma*)

Taken from atop the Williams Center Tower looking west-southwest. The main U.S. Post Office, Tulsa Police Department, and Tulsa city and county offices are all grouped in lower left-hand corner of picture. Taken at approximately 4:00 P.M. (*Courtesy of Mr. Eddie DuPree, Stillwater, Oklahoma*)

they could all discuss the issue. Four hundred fifty attended, and twenty-six spoke for or against integration and the methods available to enforce the procedure. The caucus adjourned with nothing resolved; yet the former measures that the Justice Department had sanctioned went into effect in the fall of 1972. Reactions were mixed. Many families refused to let their children leave Carver, and with their parents' aid students established Carver Freedom School. Many whites supporting integration joined black insistence to keep the school open. The board therefore obtained federal money to reopen and rechristen the old facility as Carver Middle School, which became a fulcrum for experimental learning, including individualized instruction, for initially 200 (but eventually 500) racially mixed sixth- through ninth-graders.

Federal District Judge Fred Daugherty allowed Tulsa educators to postpone the alteration of primary schools until the 1972–73 session. Daugherty further decided that five of the city's all-black buildings would remain untouched because they existed as a result

The Williams Center Tower (seen from the south at the corner of Fourth and Boston), with fifty-two floors, is the tallest building in Tulsa. Taken at approximately 4:30 P.M. (*Courtesy of Mr. Eddie DuPree, Stillwater, Oklahoma*)

of de facto rather than de jure segregation. His reasoning was that "natural" demographic shifts, such as white flight to the suburbs, had segregated the classrooms and that they were thus not unconstitutional according to *Brown* precedents. Many Tulsans continued to believe, however, that separation in all of the city schools was de jure because it was a result of the institutional racism of housing and job discrimination. Although the Justice Department filed an appeal to the district court, the latter upheld its original decision. Undaunted, 100 progressive-minded adults, eager to show federal powers and fellow Tulsans that volunteer integration could exist, met with the board of Burroughs Elementary School. From assemblies such as the first, the new Burroughs facility was born, serving seventy-nine black and ninety-eight white children.

The Metro Learning Center, located on the Washington High School campus, became another example of cooperative intermingling. In December of 1972 the Tulsa superintendent assigned administrative staff to generate a new concept, which the public debated at board meetings throughout the winter months. Recruitment to obtain students for the next fall semester finally began in March. Spokespersons went to junior and senior highs all over the city, and citizens even held socials in private homes and churches for prospective students and their parents. By fall the efforts produced a 1,100-member interracial group which participated in the most current curriculum that Tulsa schools had ever offered. The course of study had a multiplicity of electives, a highly qualified faculty, a teacher–pupil ratio of one to seventeen, and extensive career-education classes that included intern programs with local establishments.

Although federal mandates were an essential catalyst, today the nationally awarded concepts at Carver and Washington are still a functional tribute to some Tulsans' humanism. By the decade's end the board had a wealth of special programs to accommodate anywhere from 65,000 to 70,000 students. Education for handicapped, bright, and pregnant matriculants comprised part of the list; moreover, new ideas such as open-space schools, more community services, and better trades courses came into existence. The board also recognized the Tulsa Classroom Association as a faculty representative for collective bargaining and attempted to police sex discrimination in hiring practices.

While citizens and the school board wrestled with prejudice, the chamber responded to a Demonstration Agency recommendation that the city establish a junior college in which students could continue their education inexpensively. Reminiscent of the days when railroads first came to town, the chamber collected private donations for the college and lobbied at the state capitol for the right to construct the physical plant. In May of 1968 Governor Dewey Bartlett, himself from Tulsa, signed Senate Bill 493, creating Tulsa Junior College. In April of the following year the state board of regents, a governing body for all of Oklahoma's higher educational institutions, adopted the resolution, and the doors opened to 2,800 in September of 1970. Today the college has two campuses and is the largest academic two-year school in the state.

Probably the most visible sign that Tulsa was yet the land of opportunity for the rugged individualist has been among the city's educational offerings. Oral Roberts has truly portrayed a man against the system throughout his struggle to add a medical center to his already thriving undergraduate operation, Oral Roberts University. Beginning in 1978 Roberts declared that he had experienced a vision in which God had directed him to build a City of Faith teaching and healing center. He made application for the hospital branch of the envisioned healing nexus through the Oklahoma Health Planning Commission, which issued him a certificate of need; Roberts began building immediately. The Tulsa Hospital Council, however, feared the competition, because the city's already existing facilities had numerous empty beds. Its members filed suit against Roberts claiming that his undertaking was not justified, and a Tulsa district judge ruled accordingly. In the fall of 1980 Roberts announced that a giant physical manifestation of Christ had visited him and reassured the religious educator that he was fulfilling God's wishes. Taking legal as well as spiritual action, Roberts and his attorneys also appealed their case, to the Oklahoma Supreme Court, which stated in a March 1981 six-to-three decision that Tulsa had legitimate need for the additional facilities. Now Tulsans boast of having three medical schools: the University of Oklahoma Medical College, the Oklahoma Osteopathic College of Medicine and Surgery, and Oral Roberts University.

Roberts revived a pioneer frontier spirit, and the city government and Tulsa Urban Renewal Authority, with the help of federal and state monies, attempted to revitalize the progressive pride in the inner city and its cultural advantages. During 1960 the city cleared seventy-eight acres of land near the downtown area for expressways at a cost of $20 million. Buildings standing since the oil boom days gave way to a high-rise apartment building, a new shopping center, and a public center. Located between Fourth and Sixth streets added to Denver and Houston avenues, the pedestrian mall provides a place where people enjoy entertainment and lunching together. Architects proposed landscaped plazas, small parks, and a civic center plaza extending for twenty blocks, but some of the recommendations were not immediately carried out. In any case Tulsa, in 1974, won the American City Award for citizen participation progress.

The private sector has continued urban development on its own. One of the most attractive projects is the Williams Center, which houses offices of the Tulsa-based Williams companies, one firm established during early oil boom days that did not abandon the city. The complex includes the state's tallest structure, a fifty-two-

Tulsa Junior College, Metro Campus, located at 909 South Boston Avenue. This is but one of three locations in Tulsa. (*Courtesy of Mr. Eddie DuPree, Stillwater, Oklahoma*)

story Bank of Oklahoma Tower, the 400-unit Williams Plaza Hotel, and a Forum; the last houses an ice-skating rink, stores, and the Williams Center Green, an open park unattached to the forum. Two office towers complete the firm's setting, and next to it the city erected a performing arts center. Three other ambitious construction sites are either completed or close to being finished; they include the Cities Service Company building, a seven-level edifice covering an entire block; the First National Bank and Trust Company; and the State Federal Savings and Loan Association headquarters.

Other non-public concerns have renovated or are renewing older, once abandoned facilities such as Central High School, which the Public Service Company now occupies. In addition Reading and Baites Corporation restored the Mid-Continent edifice and is adding to it a thirty-two-story terra cotta skyscraper. In an attempt to elevate the commercially depressed north side, the chamber of commerce has sponsored the Industries for Tulsa organization and

New City of Faith Hospital complex, located directly south of the main ORU Campus at the corner of south Sixty-first and Lewis. The tower is sixty stories tall. A pair of praying hands are directly in front of the complex and is roughly sixty feet tall. (*Courtesy of Mr. Eddie DuPree, Stillwater, Oklahoma*)

is currently promoting a Cherokee Expressway Industrial District, a 1,400-acre plot located on the city's north side. Several business concerns have already purchased land, but the project's future remains unforetold.

Rejuvenation and expansion have created urban transit difficulties. By the mid-1960s the city ranked second in the nation in automobiles per capita, exceeded only by Los Angeles, and traffic congestion was rapidly becoming quite dangerous. Authorized personnel spent $5 million in 1960 alone for street repairs and two years later constructed fifty-three miles of new pavement, expended $1,464,854 for a new expressway and added six miles of sidewalks to the downtown area. Even with the emphasis on speeding, though, traffic flow into and out of the city has caused streets and highways to remain overcrowded. A second problem of inadequate water distribution and treatment facilities is a chronic concern. The city therefore is currently pushing for inception of a regional water authority.

Despite economic progress, inner-city vagrancy has persisted. To help the destitute, the chamber and a group called Downtown Tulsa, Unlimited have inspired the creation of a "booze cruiser" which motors around the inner city picking up drunks and transporting them to a psychological help center called Second Chance, Incorporated. Usually around forty persons live there and receive assistance at any given time.

Despite any encumbrances, Tulsa civic leaders have made every effort to generate fiscal growth and stability throughout the seventies. City commissioners formed the Economic Development Commission (EDC) to tout Tulsa as a garden spot for business, tourism, conventions, and trade shows. The organization obtained promotional funds from a five-cent hotel/motel room tax. The EDC's 1980 budget, more than $1 million, was an indication of the prodigious resources available.

It has been no wonder that despite national portents of economic hard times, Tulsa leaders have continued to exude the optimism of early-day boosters. In a 1981 speech presented at the Oklahoma State Chamber Board, William M. Waller, EDC chairman, hailed the city's comparatively excellent commercial conditions. He reported that unemployment was just over 3 percent, less than half the national average. Waller continued:

McFarlin Library, located on the main entrance to Tulsa University Campus, at 600 College Drive. The view is looking from the west. (*Courtesy of Mr. Eddie DuPree, Stillwater, Oklahoma*)

The McDonnell Douglas complex, located on the southeast corner of the Tulsa International Airport. Such projects as NASA's Space Shuttle and the new B-1 Bomber project are done at this facility. The view is from the west at the end of the north-south runway. Taken at about 6:05 P.M. (*Courtesy of Mr. Eddie DuPree, Stillwater, Oklahoma*)

> Second quarter 1981 retail sales were up twenty-five percent over the same period last year. June 1981 bank loan balances for large Tulsa region banks reporting to the Federal Reserve were up twenty and eight-tenths percent last year, and deposits were up eleven and six-tenths for the same period.

The speaker further boasted, "The value of commercial building permits within the Tulsa city limits during 1981's first six months was $183,000,000, 10 percent more than those issued for all of 1980." He reported that while Tulsa's population nationally ranked only thirty-eighth, in 1981's first quarter the city was twenty-first in the value of building certificates. Much of the new space has been for offices belonging to new companies that the EDC hopes to lure, Waller concluded.

Throughout Tulsa's modern era a majority of voters have adhered to Republicanism in national elections. The city voted for Richard Nixon three times in four presidential contests and for Senator Barry Goldwater against President Johnson. Democrat James Maxwell, though, defeated mayoral nominees from the Republican Party in three more successful bids between 1960 and 1964. The city chief executive also bested his primary challengers in 1966 and ran for his fifth term, but Republican oil man James M. Hewgley won by 5,000 votes. The GOP has remained in power to 1980. Robert LaFortune first won in 1968 and held his post until Republican James Inhofe squeezed by Rodger Randle; then in 1980 Inhofe won more dramatically, beating Richard Johnson by more than 23,000 votes out of 75,714 cast.

In 1930 Tulsans emerged from a nationally liberal era with a stubborn commitment to self-reliance and Republicanism. Aside from their preachments, however, throughout the sixties and seventies they displayed a penchant for working in concert toward economic and educational progress—the very quality that built their town. As the formerly mentioned company chairman Williams has stated, many Tulsans believe it their legacy not only to stimulate economic well-being, but to carry on progressive reforms from which all residents can benefit.

American Airlines' major aircraft repair and service center, located on the east side of the Tulsa Airport. It is also their training center for stewardesses and stewards. Taken at about 6:10 P.M. (*Courtesy of Mr. Eddie DuPree, Stillwater, Oklahoma*)

IX

The Urban Frontier: Past, Present, and Future

Like the stereotypic sojourner in the Turner scenario, most Tulsans came to the Osage Hills in search of economic prosperity and a better tomorrow; yet they soon realized that they would not succeed within a chaotic environment. Settlers therefore busily created an environment quite similar to the one they left behind, except this time the newcomers were in charge. Trail of Tears survivors, traditional antebellum Tallahassee Creeks, saw white encroachment as the enemy; yet mixed-blood Indians believed that wedding their interests to the champions of farming and (after the Civil War) ranching was an excellent idea. They might then benefit from the by-products of modernization generated in eastern and northern cities. The Protestant missionaries, moreover, although themselves loners, facilitated Creek assimilation into a capitalistic Anglo culture through academic and Christian education.

Late nineteenth-century Tulsa stockmen eagerly supplied beef and other staples to the industrialized Midwest, the Atlantic Seaboard, and the South. They also made attempts to erect a school and begin organizations such as the Masonic Lodge and cattlemen's associations, which were symbols of a collective, not an anarchistic, world. The railroad was the harbinger of disaster only for separatist Creeks, but for other men and women it was a precious link that lined their pockets with money.

Scholar Gerald D. Nash indicates that approximately two-thirds of the twentieth-century trans-Mississippi settlers live in commercial centers, partly because of the dry conditions in many regions.* Like these other westerners, during the twentieth century Tulsans manifested their need for designing a city. Throughout the early 1900s they fostered municipal growth by founding the Commercial Club and later the chamber of commerce for the express purpose of luring business, especially oil concerns, to Tulsa. Members knew that only by cooperation could they build a community. To accommodate the burgeoning town the chamber and city government madly built roads and public facilities. When aviation pioneers portended the airplane's future during the first decades of the century, some precocious Tulsans began a campaign that eventually raised millions of dollars to construct airport facilities and coax major airlines to land in Tulsa. The Arkansas River Navigation System was another result of the quest for modern transportation to and from the city, and it solidified bonds with the rest of the nation on land, by water, and in the air. No longer was Tulsa a colony of the older states, but a modern city quite similar to northern prototypes.

Many Tulsans also supported the progressive social movement that took place in cities throughout the country during the first two decades of the twentieth century. Men and women brought symphonic music, education, thespian arts, painting, and sculpture within their reach. Later the Gilcrease Museum/Library and the Philbrook Art Center illustrated Tulsans' hunger for learning and culture and carried on a tradition that progressive ancestors began with early Hyechka Club activities.

Although public spirit made a city out of a quiet Indian village, we cannot leave the impression that individualism or conservatism was not ingrained in Tulsans' social fabric. As Richard Hofstadter has pointed out, the first progressives were not liberals in spirit, although they may have relied on government intervention and

*Nash further states that the majority of westerners settled in communities during the nineteenth century, as well. Within the states of Idaho, Wyoming, and Montana demographics illustrate an exception to the regional fact.

planning. Instead they were white, middle-class people who believed that America once offered opportunity, but that the loss of free land and growth in population had limited the chance for success. The reformers therefore reasoned that if people controlled robber barons' greed, then the average citizen could enjoy technological and scientific treasures beyond his imagination. Through cooperative strides to break up monopolies, produce plays, or build industries, to name only a few, Tulsa founders and protectors sought to insure, not destroy, personal advancement, and there were always "rags-to-riches" stories which assured leaders that they were succeeding. Families such as the Perrymans or the Clintons made fortunes in cattle and oil, respectively; moreover, a former revivalist orator named Oral Roberts created an educational and religious empire in Tulsa.

Unrest has also reared its head and illustrated that if Tulsa was a Turnerian western safety valve for eastern urban conflict, then Tulsa inherited what it prevented elsewhere. Migrants with thwarted dreams of material success often fomented flagrant lawlessness, which was a persistent problem, from the ruthless federal Indian agents to the post–Civil War-era gangs, which, out of fear, townspeople often harbored. During the 1920s Klan terrorism, usually generated by frustrated poor whites, turned on blacks and organized labor as if to say, "There's not room enough for all of us!" Finally, the twenties race riot and proletariat demands suggested that Tulsa was not an oasis for some seekers whose mobility ladder had fallen to the ground. The outbursts, however, were always subdued and institutionalized within the lexicon of independence, which imbued Tulsa politicians' rhetoric.

Both Democrats and Republicans expressed the average person's fear of national government encroachment into his or her life, although city powerhouses and common citizens alike welcomed collective responses to local problems. Tulsans accepted federally subsidized railroads in the 1880s, New Deal relief/recovery money from 1932 through the 1940s, and Great Society doles in the 1960s that made urban renewal, educational, and the Arkansas River navigation projects possible. Although many Indian and white Tulsans supported slavery and then segregation after the Civil War, when called to task during the sixties they worked as a community to create a few outstanding integrated public-school facilities.

Both nineteenth- and twentieth-century travelers have not been able to resist the inviting climate, which cradles sandstone hills that converge with lush bluestem and switchgrass. The restful shade of a pecan, black walnut, or cottonwood tree is too pleasant to pass by; and so Tulsa continues to grow. Settlers, however, have always felt compelled to do more than nestle in and appreciate the surroundings; instead, they have molded and manipulated the landscape, producing oil-well derricks and skyscrapers to resemble not nature's, but man's, concept of a fulfilling, fruitful existence–the city. Hopefully residents will recall the collective spirit, made up from socially-conscious persons, which built and sustained their city, while the future confronts them with industrial pollution, persistent needs for updated educational curriculums, and ever present demands from the oppressed who cry out for a piece of the Western American Dream.

SOURCE NOTES

We have not attempted to list all of the sources used for this work. The following are materials that might guide another scholar conducting further research. Tulsa has not drawn historians' attention as have Kansas City, Denver, or major West-Coast cities; thus there were few secondary sources on our topic, but a plethora of so-called primary sources existed. Throughout the book we relied especially upon Angie Debo, *From Creek Town to Oil Capital* (1943); Clarence B. Douglas, *The History of Tulsa, a City With a Personality* (1921); and James M. Hall, *The Beginning of Tulsa* (1933). For a highly entertaining and colorful account we read William Butler, *Tulsa 75: A History of Tulsa* (1975). Other principal resources were the *Tulsa Daily Democrat, Tulsa Tribune*, the *Tulsa Daily World*, and *Harlow's Weekly* newspapers.

CHAPTER I

For a summary of the concept that the frontier created individualistic persons see Frederick Jackson Turner, *The Frontier in American History* (1920).

Stanley Elkins and Erick McKitrick first postulated their belief that boosterism unified frontier community existence in "A Meaning for Turner's Frontier," *Political Science Quarterly* 69 (1954). Although their ideas reflect a Turnerian proposition, they emphasized town building, not individualism, as the rugged response to a challenging environment. Allan Bogue, "Social Theory and the Pioneer," *Agricultural History* 34 (1960) and Robert Dykstra, *The Cattle Towns* (1968) present a conflict frame of reference within which to judge western settlements. Don Harrison Doyle, *The Social Order of a Frontier Community: Jacksonville, Illinois, 1825–70* (1978) leans toward the conflict theory, but concludes that a social order eventually developed out of the controversy between individualism and communalism.

CHAPTER II

For materials on Tulsa's Creek beginnings we used Angie Debo, *From Creek Town to Oil Capital* (1943) and Debo, *The Road to Disappearance* (1941). The Creek peoples' history before removal was covered in Ohland Norton, "Early History of the Creek Indians," *Chronicles of Oklahoma* IX (1951), and "The Government of the Creek Indians," *Chronicles of Oklahoma* VIII (1930). For interesting descriptions of Creek law and relations with neighboring tribes we depended on John R. Swanton, *Early History of the Creek Indians and Their Neighbors* (1922); Antonio J. Waring (ed.), *Laws of the Creek Nation* (1960); and Charles J. Kappler (ed.), *Indian Affairs: Laws and Treaties*, II (1904).

Vivid portrayals of the Civil War in the Indian Territory and around Tulsa were in LeRoy H. Fisher (ed.), *The Civil War Era in Indian Territory* (1974) and Gail Bolman, "The Creek Treaty of 1866," *Chronicles of Oklahoma* XXXVIII (1970).

For details surrounding missionary work, especially in the field of education, we focused on Charles E. Noland (ed.), "Recollections of Tulsa, Indian Territory, From Sister Mary Agnes Newchurch, O. Carm.," *Chronicles of Oklahoma* XLIX (1971). Also helpful were Sister Mary Urban Kehoe, C.D.P., "The Educational Activities of Distinguished Catholic Missionaries Among the Five Civilized Tribes," *Chronicles of Oklahoma* XXIV (1946), and the works of Virginia E. Lauderdale, "Tallahassee Mission," *Chronicles of Oklahoma* XXVI (1948), and Lila Denton Lindsey,

"Memories of the Indian Territory Mission Field," *Chronicles of Oklahoma* XXXVI (1958).

Biographical sketches of the community leaders by John B. Meserve, "The McIntoshes," *Chronicles of Oklahoma* X (1932), and "The Perrymans," *Chronicles of Oklahoma* V (1937), made many frontier facts come to life.

CHAPTER III

The general setting for the ranching around the Tulsa area was realistically depicted in Walter Prescott Webb, *The Great Plains* (1931) and Henry Nash Smith, *Virgin Land: The American West As Symbol and Myth* (1950). For a close look at Tulsa, in particular, we read Norman A. Graebner, "Cattle Ranching in Eastern Oklahoma," *Chronicles of Oklahoma* XXI (1943), and Joseph G. McCoy and Ralph Bieber, *Historic Sketches of the Cattle Trade of the West and Southwest* (1940). J. Evetts Haley, *Charles Goodnight, Cowman and Plainsman* (1949) had lively stories involving the cattle business. Ella M. Robinson, "The Daugherty Ranch, Creek Nation," *Chronicles of Oklahoma* XLVII (1960); James M. Hall, *The Beginnings of Tulsa* (1933); and R. M. McClintock, "Tulsa–A Story of Achievement," *Tulsa Tribune* (1924), included interesting biographical notations. The single most valuable piece was the oral history by Grant Foreman, *Indian–Pioneer History* (1937). The Dawes Commission Files located in the Indian Archives section of the Oklahoma Historical Society detailed the final dissolution of Indian Territory into the state of Oklahoma. The best research on the Dawes Commission's political origins was in two articles by Loren N. Brown, "The Dawes Commission," *Chronicles of Oklahoma* IX (1931), and "The Establishment of the Dawes Commission for Indian Territory," *Chronicles of Oklahoma* XVIII (1940).

CHAPTER IV

Information about the early petroleum industry in Oklahoma came largely from local newspapers, especially the *Indian Journal* printed in Muskogee, Oklahoma, and the *Tulsa Daily Democrat*. Two invaluable books were Carl Coke Rister, *Oil! Titan of the Southwest* (1949) and Anthony Sampson, *The Seven Sisters: The Great Oil Companies and the World They Made* (1975).

Facts about early petroleum discoveries around Tulsa were in Muriel Wright, "First Oklahoma Oil Was Produced in 1859," *Chronicles of Oklahoma* IV (1926); S. G. Bayne, *Derricks of Destiny* (1924); and Wilbur F. Cloud, *Petroleum Production* (1937). The best knowledge about the Glenn Pool area came from C. B. Glasscock, *Then Came Oil* (1938), and for a more personal perspective we called on W. L. Connelly, *The Oil Business*

As I Saw It (1954) and Max W. Ball, *This Fascinating Oil Business* (1940). James Leonard Bates best related the crusade for government regulation in his *The Origins of Tea Pot Dome: Progressives, Parties, and Petroleum, 1909–1921* (1963). The Red Fork strike data stemmed from the pen of leading early-Tulsa oil man Fred S. Clinton, "First Oil and Gas Well in Tulsa County," *Chronicles of Oklahoma* XX (1952). Two final works developed the way in which the Tulsa petroleum industry changed. They were William Butler, *Tulsa '75* (1975) and in the American Guide Series, *Tulsa, A Guide to the Oil Capital* (1940).

CHAPTER V

We discovered the best general urban history on the American West was Gerald Nash, *The American West in the Twentieth Century: A Short History of an Urban Oasis* (1974). A guideline for researching our book hailed from A. Theodore Brown and Lyle W. Dorsett, *K. C. A History of Kansas City, Missouri* (1978) and Lyle W. Dorsett, *The Queen City: A History of Denver* (1977). We also learned much about how to study the leaders of the Tulsa community from reading Reid Holland, "Urban Frontier Leadership," PhD dissertation, Oklahoma State University (1971).

The best biographies came from articles such as Charles Evans, "Harry Campbell," *Chronicles of Oklahoma* XXVIII (1950), and Louise Morse Whitman, "Fred Severs Clinton, M.D., F.A.C.S.," *Chronicles of Oklahoma* XXXIII (1955), which painted brief sketches of two businessmen, Harry Campbell and Fred Clinton. Harry Campbell, "Reminiscences," *Chronicles of Oklahoma* XXVII (1950), had a variety of insights from one of the early twentieth-century migrants. A portrait of "Tulsa's First Lady," Jane Heard Clinton, was the theme of Angie Debo, "Jane Heard Clinton," *Chronicles of Oklahoma* XXIV (1946). C. B. Douglas, *The History of Tulsa* (1921) also told of other persons' contributions.

The Minutes of the Directors' Meetings of the chamber of commerce convinced us that "boosterism" was not peculiar to Tulsa but certainly exemplified its personality, especially from 1900 to 1920. In addition we looked to the Tulsa ordinance files in city hall for constructing the demographic development of the town during the period.

CHAPTER VI

The role Tulsans played in the first World War was well recounted in William T. Lampe's (comp.) *Tulsa County in the World War* (1919). The anti-foreign attitudes were explained in James H. Fowler, "Extralegal Suppression of Civil Liberties in Oklahoma During the First World War," M. A. thesis, Oklahoma State University (1974).

The famous race riot coupled with a Ku Klux Klan resurrection set the tone for the social and political climate during the years preceding the second World War. A good general study of race conditions in Tulsa since 1900 came from the National Urban League, *A Study of the Social and Economic Conditions of the Negro Population of Tulsa, Oklahoma: A Community Relations Project of the Tulsa Council of Social Agencies* (1946). We took the most gripping account of the violence itself from Loren L. Gill, "The Tulsa Race Riot," M. A. thesis, University of Tulsa (1946). For a more contemporary analysis we digested George E. Hayes, "Race Riots in Relation to Democracy," *Survey* XLII (1919). We easily followed in the local press Tulsa Klan activities and Governor Bill Walton's fight against the society. Two articles, by McAlister Coleman, "When the Troops Took Tulsa," *The Nation* XVII (1923), and Howard Tucker, *History of Governor Walton's War on the Ku Klux Klan* (1924), outlined the reasons that Governor Walton felt compelled to declare martial law in Tulsa.

We especially depended upon John David Hoff, "A History of Tulsa International Airport," M. A. thesis, University of Tulsa (1967), and Glenn O. Hopkins, "Spartan School of Aeronautics–Tulsa," *Chronicles of Oklahoma* XXVII (1949), to analyze commercial growth during the 1920s. Without a doubt the largest public-relations event of the decade was the beginning of the International Petroleum Exposition. For the story of its conception we utilized *The Official Records of the International Petroleum Exposition, Incorporated, Minute Book and Book of By-Laws 1923–1940,* and Public Relations Department, *International Petroleum Exposition: The History of the Tulsa Oil Show 1923–1958, A Report Prepared by the Public Relations Department* (1958). Finally, R. M. McClintock, "Tulsa–A Story of Achievement," *Tulsa Tribune* (July 31, 1924), assessed industrial development after the first World War.

CHAPTER VII

The Great Depression had a dramatic impact on Tulsa, as it did on the rest of the nation. The tragedy aggravated the normal problems incurred when a local economy depended on one product (oil), a point made throughout "How Tulsa Will Expend $6,230,000 To Carry Out Its City Commissioners' Recommendations," *The American City* XLII (1930); the Tulsa Chamber of Commerce, *Industrial Employment Survey Bulletin, 1921–1930* (1931). Efforts to implement New Deal programs proved mixed, as explained in Reid Holland, "The Civilian Conservation Corps in Oklahoma," M. A. thesis, Oklahoma State University (1968); and John Joseph Mathews, *Life and Death of an Oil Man: The Career of E. W. Marland* (1951). City efforts to fight a weakening economy had at best mixed results, according to the "Annual Reports of the Engineering Department of the City of Tulsa" (1936), and the City Auditor's "Monthly Report" located in the Tulsa Municipal Building. "The Minutes of the Directors' Meeting: Report of the Fact-Finding Committee" (October 25, 1931) elaborated on chamber of commerce endeavors to combat Depression results. Census data and Francis Dominic Burke, "A Survey of the Negro Community of Tulsa, Oklahoma," M. A. thesis, University of Oklahoma (1936), substantiated the effects of hard times on the economically disadvantaged.

Throughout the 1930s Tulsans and their fellow Oklahomans often expressed anti–New Deal sentiments. No work illustrated this attitude better than two publications by Governor William H. Murray, *Memoirs of Governor Murray* (1945) and *Essays on Forms of Government From Theocracy to Foolocracy* (1942).

CHAPTER VIII

The most productive assessments of Tulsa and Oklahoma during the second World War included Arrell M. Gibson, *Oklahoma: A History of Five Centuries* (1965) and Edwin C. McReynolds, *Oklahoma: A History of the Sooner State* (1951). No study of Tulsa except ours existed during the war years and thereafter. Again, we learned from the *Tulsa Tribune* and *Tulsa World* newspapers. We also profitably went through city government publications such as *Land Utilization and Marketability Study, Riverview Park Urban Renewal Project* (1965) on economic expansion since the second World War.

Historians have ignored the metamorphosis of Tulsa's educational system. Conditions in the public school system immediately after the war such as poor working conditions, segregated, unequal facilities, and low administrator and teacher salaries were disclosed in "The New Salary Schedule for Tulsa Educators," *Tulsa School Review* V (1948); "Classes at Night Help Busy Adults Earn Promotions," *Tulsa School Review* V (1949); and "1949 School Census Shows 1,802 Gain in Tulsa District Over Last Report," *Tulsa School Review* V (1949). Steps to ameliorate the situation were condensed from Tulsa Board of Education minutes and presented in "Tulsa Public Schools," *In No Time at All* (1976).

For materials reenacting politics during the post-war period we centered upon the local newspapers, the Bureau of Government Research at the University of Oklahoma, *Oklahoma Votes, 1907–1962* (1964), and the State of Oklahoma, *Directory of the State of Oklahoma*, published annually for a county voter analysis of local, state, and national elections.

CHAPTER IX

The most comprehensive financial figures since 1960 originated from City of Tulsa, Oklahoma, *Land Utilization and Marketability Study* (1965) and John Pierce, "Business Highlights, 2nd Quarter, 1975," *Tulsa* LII (1975). The most celebrated happening since 1960 has been the Arkansas River Waterway System. Recreating comprehensive details required a perusal of United States Congress, Committee on Flood Control, *Control of the Destructive Flood Waters of the United States,* 70th Congress, 1st Session (1927–28). Early thoughts on the scheme were registered in "Steaming Up To Tulsey Town," *Tulsa Spirit* (1929); and Theodore Brent, *A Report on the Arkansas River Waterway for the Mississippi Valley Association* (1931). For the most persuasive case favoring the project we considered State of Oklahoma, *The States of Arkansas and Oklahoma Present Additional Benefits in the Proposed Comprehensive Improvement of the Arkansas River Basin: Submitted to Major General Eugene Reybald, Chief of Engineers, United States Army* (1945) and Col. Clayton B. Lyle, "Navigation on the Arkansas River," *Interstate Pat Handbook,* 32nd edition (1966).

Tulsa had a special reputation for its beautiful downtown area, which urban renewal funds made possible. Key works that underscored Tulsans' dedication to keeping their city attractive were City of Tulsa, Oklahoma, *City Demonstration Agency, Tulsa Model Cities Program: A Comprehensive Demonstration Program To Improve the Quality of Urban Life* (1969), and Tulsa Urban Renewal Authority, *Downtown Northwest: An Urban Renewal Project for Tulsa, Oklahoma* (1968). In addition, interviews concerning urban renewal with Bruce Carnett and Joseph Williams were most helpful. Selected economic data came from William M. Waller, "Suggested Remarks," Oklahoma State Chamber Board Meeting (August 27, 1981), and material on Tulsa racism came from Joseph H. Williams, " Remarks at Luncheon Session," Symposium on Inner-City Economic Development (Tulsa, Oklahoma, 1980).

CHAPTER X

The theoretical framework used to prove that Tulsa's history was rooted in progressive thought derived from the masterful work of David W. Noble, *The Progressive Mind, 1890–1917* (1970). Noble postulated that Progressives believed the Turnerian concept that the frontier had been the foundation for American democracy and a chance for all to make a good living. Our theory that Tulsa leaders were also individualistic and conservative was not incongruous, according to Richard Hofstadter, *The American Political Tradition and the Men Who Made It* (1948), who said that progressives were in fact conservative. We are also indebted to our contemporaries, especially Danney Goble for his work *Progressive Oklahoma: The Making of a New Kind of State* (1980), in which he defined progressivism and demonstrated that, at least during the statehood years, Oklahoma shared the same belief that the American Dream of equal opportunity must be constantly enforced through cooperative programs and government regulation.

INDEX